General editor

Peter

Herriot

Essential

Psychology

Instinct,
Environment
and
Behaviour

S.E.G. Lea

Instinct, Environment and Behaviour

Methuen

London and New York

First published in 1984 by
Methuen & Co. Ltd
11 New Fetter Lane, London EC4P 4EE

Published in the USA by
Methuen & Co.
in association with Methuen, Inc.
733 Third Avenue, New York, NY 10017

Typeset by Rowland Phototypesetting Ltd
Printed in Great Britain by
Richard Clay (The Chaucer Press) Ltd
Bungay, Suffolk

British Library
Cataloguing in Publication Data

Lea, S.E.G.
Instinct, environment and
behaviour.—(New essential psychology)
1. Psychology, Physiological
I. Title   II. Series
152   QP360

ISBN 0-416-33640-X

Library of Congress
Cataloging in Publication Data

Lea, S.E.G., 1946–
Instinct, environment and behaviour.
(New essential psychology)
Bibliography: p.
Includes index.
1. Psychology, Comparative.
2. Psychobiology.
I. Title.   II. Series.
BF671.L42   1983   156   83-17308

ISBN 0-416-33640-X (pbk.)

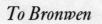

To Bronwen

Contents

Preface

The aim of this book is to introduce the biological approach to the study of behaviour. It forms part of a series addressed to people studying psychology, and so I have tried not to assume any background of biological knowledge. Because ethology is often studied at the beginning of a psychology course, I have not assumed any detailed knowledge of psychology either, so I hope that the book will be useful to students of psychology and biology alike, and indeed to anyone, student or not, who is interested in how animals behave and what that can tell us about human behaviour.

A biological approach does, inevitably, imply a study of animal behaviour. My aim is to give the reader a general understanding of behaviour, and the way it works, which can be applied to all species of animals – not to offer an explanation of human behaviour in terms of what gulls, rats or chimpanzees do. But the amount of information available on animal behaviour is now very great indeed, and I have had to select both the examples I have used and even the topics I have considered. In making my selection, I have tried to emphasize the problems that are most important to human life; in fact the whole book can be seen as an attempt to answer one question: from a behavioural point of view, are human beings a special case or do we fit into the general pattern of the animal kingdom?

As an academic subdiscipline, the study of animal behaviour is relatively new. One of the charms of the first generation of textbooks on the subject is that the authors wrote mostly about what they had seen at first hand; they were truly experts on the species they described. The explosion of literature on behaviour that has taken place over the past twenty-five years means that no one could write a fairly representative textbook and still describe only behaviours they had seen for themselves. That would be true even of the greatest of our ethologists, let alone of someone like me who is primarily a psychologist seeking to interpret the literature on animal behaviour for my own psychological purposes. The present book lacks not only the freshness of first-hand observations but also the vividness of illustration. I have tried to do something to rectify both deficiencies by picking examples, wherever possible, from the behaviour of species that are easily observed, either because they are kept as domestic, farm or zoo animals, or (with apologies to non-British readers) because they are common British wild species. The best 'further reading' readers can do is to look around at the animals that share their particular world, and try to see the behaviours described here as they actually occur.

Although this is an introductory book, I have tried to give full references for every fact that is mentioned. These are there so that you can, if you wish, check that every 'fact' mentioned really is a fact, and find out just how good a fact it is. Most readers should simply ignore them.

Academic colleagues reading this book will recognize many of my debts. Successive editions of Manning's *An Introduction to Animal Behaviour* have been my constant resource as a teacher of ethology, and this book is not intended to supplant that admirable text, rather to supplement it at a rather less detailed level. I intend the same relationship to Dawkins' endlessly stimulating *The Selfish Gene*. And like everyone working on behaviour, I owe a debt which can never be repaid to the great reference texts, E.O. Wilson's *Sociobiology* and R.A. Hinde's *Animal Behaviour*. To

Robert Hinde I owe rather more, for I caught my interest in ethology in his undergraduate lectures at Cambridge, as the general structure of the present work no doubt bears witness.

Other debts are less obvious. This book grew out of a course of lectures I gave for several years to a very mixed group of undergraduates at the University of Exeter. As they were taking psychology as an ancillary subject, their main interests spanned the academic spectrum, from philosophy to biology by way of chemistry, computer science and statistics. The one thing they had in common was a willingness to be interested if given half a chance; the selection of material in this book owes a lot to their enthusiasms and criticisms. I am also very grateful to a number of friends, Tracey Adams, Mary Gill, Mark MacNair, Kathryn Parker, Catriona Ryan and Paul Webley, who read early drafts and pointed out innumerable errors and obscurities. My greatest debt, in this as in everything I do, is expressed in the dedication.

S.E.G. LEA

1

A biological approach to behaviour

When you are reading a play, do you skip over the list of characters at the beginning, and the instructions for setting the scene? If so, you probably shouldn't read this chapter. It tries to explain what the rest of the book is about.

My aim in this book is to introduce the biological approach to behaviour, usually called 'ethology'. Anyone who uses this approach can be called an 'ethologist', though there are several different kinds of ethologist, with different approaches and interests. 'Ethology' just means the study of behaviour, but it has come to refer particularly to the way of studying behaviour that treats it as a biological entity. Often, it involves looking at the behaviour of animals other than human beings. Although many psychologists would say they study behaviour, they would not usually call themselves ethologists. In effect, ethology is the study of behaviour seen as part of zoology rather than, say, part of social science or philosophy.

Why does ethology matter? The next few sections of this chapter give my answer to this basic question.

Why does behaviour matter in biology?

In the course of this century there has been a sharp increase in the proportion of the total biological effort devoted to behaviour. Why is this? Is it simply a shift of fashion, or the scientific community catching up on a neglected area? Or is there some more fundamental reason? It seems to me that there is, and that it is quite simple. In this century, biology has had what it did not have before, a coherent theoretical basis. That basis is Darwin's theory of evolution by natural selection. This theory is so basic to all biology that anything which matters to natural selection matters to biology. And behaviour matters, crucially, to natural selection. Let us see why this is so.

Vertebrate life began in water. At some point, we suppose, something a little like a modern lungfish became adapted to survive the occasional drying out of the pools it lived in. That much could have been a purely physiological adaptation, but it would have had no interesting evolutionary consequences if there had not also been a change in behaviour: the animal started to move around on dry land, feeding or avoiding predators. From that crucial behavioural step all land vertebrates spring. Without it, there would have been no reason for that primitive proto-amphibian to develop anything more than a capacity to survive, passively, out of water for a shorter or longer time.

Almost all other interesting evolutionary developments have a behavioural component in the same sort of way. In terms of evolution, changes in behaviour and changes in anatomical structure or physiological capacity go hand in hand. It is this evolutionary fact that gives behaviour its central importance in modern biology. It also makes it inevitable that a biological approach to behaviour will be an evolutionary approach.

Why does a biological approach matter in psychology?

Why should anyone except a biologist be interested in an evolutionary approach to behaviour? After all, many readers of this book will be psychologists rather than biologists, or lay people not committed to any discipline. Why should the evolution of behaviour matter to them?

The first reason is a negative one. We have to be interested because so many people have been in the past. Explanations and justifications of human behaviour in terms of our supposed evolutionary past, in terms of what other animals from rats and pigeons through geese and gulls to chimpanzees do – these abound in both the popular and the scientific literature. If this book can correct some of the wilder speculations that are at present in circulation, it will have more than served its turn.

More positively, though, an evolutionary explanation is often a plausible starter as a way of accounting for behaviour. Take a contentious example, the tendency for men to be more aggressive than women. Male aggressiveness is an obvious general tendency throughout almost all vertebrates. It may or may not be the case that male humans are aggressive for the same reasons as male chimpanzees, male rats and male mallards; but if we can understand the functions and mechanisms of male aggression in mallards, rats and chimpanzees (and we can), we at least have some hypotheses to start testing in the human case.

But the simplest, and for me the most important, reason for being interested in the evolutionary account of behaviour is simply that we cannot understand what it is to be human unless we know what it is to be other than human. There is no doubt that the human species is unique, if only because every species is unique, but unless we know quite a lot about the other species of animal that share our world, we are likely to be gravely mistaken about the precise nature of human uniqueness.

Four ways of applying the biology of behaviour

Understanding animal behaviour therefore seems to me to be an essential part of understanding ourselves. That is a somewhat rarefied reason for being interested in ethology, however. Are there any more practical gains to be expected from studying animal behaviour? I see four ways in which ethology is an applied science.

The first is limited in scope but is not open to serious dispute. Human beings have to interact with animals in a variety of ways. On farms, in zoos and in wildlife reserves, animals have to be managed, for our purposes and often also for their own good. It should not need arguing that a knowledge of their behaviour can make for better husbandry. An obvious example involves mating behaviours in endangered species: there are many species that will not survive the next few decades unless they can be induced to breed in captivity or near captivity, and unless we know quite a bit about their normal mating procedures, we may be unable to provide the right conditions for that to happen.

A second relatively uncontroversial application of ethology is the use of its experimental and observational *methods*, originally developed for use with animals, in the study of human behaviour. There has been a spate of this so-called 'human ethology' in the past decade, and some of it at least has been both novel and interesting. We shall see that the ethologist's chief methodological tool is close and detailed observation, and this has also character-ized the human ethologists' work. A few psychologists may find the introduction of ethological methods and terminology gim-micky or even threatening, but on the whole this kind of applica-tion of ethology is working well, especially in studies of babies and young children.

The third way of applying ethology is closely linked to the second, but is much more controversial. It involves taking over *ideas* and concepts developed in ethology and incorporating them into psychological theory. There have been some successful transplants along these lines. For example, the concept of 'indi-vidual distance', the distance which two individuals of the same species always try to keep between each other, started in Hediger's analysis of the behaviour of zoo animals, but (under the alias of 'personal space') it has now acquired a key place within social and environmental psychology. When we look at real examples like this, though, we find that there is not and should not be any automatic acceptance of ethological ideas within psychology. It is only if those ideas prove themselves useful, when tested against human, psychological data, that they are taken up and developed within the mainstream of psychology.

The last and most questionable way of applying ethology is the direct extrapolation of *results* from studies of animal behaviour to human affairs. It is an immensely attractive game, which any number can play. Robert Ardrey, Desmond Morris, even such paramount figures as Konrad Lorenz and E.O. Wilson, all have published popular or semi-popular books trying to make this kind of extrapolation. It goes on in the sober-sided learned journals as well. It is good fun, for authors and readers alike. It may suggest all

4

sorts of testable hypotheses; it may also raise all sorts of hackles, and both those are often useful things to do. But they are not, in themselves, science, and they should not be allowed to cloak themselves in scientific respectability. They are not science fiction either, but something in between; science myth, perhaps.

Such speculation is quite harmless so long as people recognize it for what it is. There is a certain amount of it in this book, because it is almost impossible to resist the temptation to draw analogies from what we know about animal behaviour to what we should like to explain about human behaviour. But I have tried to let it be clear when I am stopping being scientific and offering a little fun.

Key concepts of evolutionary theory

I have said that a biological approach to behaviour is bound to be an evolutionary approach. That is in any case what we usually want when we are considering applying ethology to human affairs: evolution offers us answers to some of our most profound questions about ourselves, the questions that begin, 'Why . . . ?' Why are men more aggressive than women? Why do we smile when we are pleased and frown when we are angry? Why do we, alone among animals, speak? We have seen that we need to be cautious in applying ethology to answer such questions, but that does not mean we should make no attempt to find answers at all.

But if we are going to give evolution a central role in our thinking, we had better make sure that we are operating with the genuine article, not with some half-understood misrepresentation of Darwin's theory. Almost everyone knows roughly what the theory of evolution says, but there are several ways in which that rough understanding needs to be polished up if we are to make sense of either animal or human behaviour.

The first step is to be clear about the meanings of words. 'Evolution' just means gradual rather than sudden formation: Darwin meant that species are formed from other species by a series of linked steps, rather than springing forth from nowhere, or from the hand of God, in the form in which we now see them. By the phrase 'natural selection', Darwin meant that there are natural processes that operate in the same way as human breeders do, perpetuating some lines in preference to others and so producing new varieties of animal. A common way of talking about natural selection is to refer to 'the survival of the fittest'; nowadays, this is simply treated as a definition of 'fitness'. To a biologist, a relatively 'fit' animal is simply one that leaves more descendants than some other animal of the same species (which is therefore relatively less fit).

So much for the basic terms of the theory. A few other words crop up so often that they need to be explained here. 'Adaptedness' is the property of being well suited to the environment an organism lives in. It does not mean the same as 'fitness'. The better adapted an animal is, the fitter it is likely to be, but it is possible to be fit without being well adapted, and well adapted without being fit – it all depends on what competition there is. The precise environment to which an animal is adapted is called its 'ecological niche'; a law formulated by Gause (1934) states that no two species can occupy the same niche. A 'selective pressure' is any property of the environment, particularly any property of the ecological niche, that tends to favour one form of a species rather than a different form of the same species; that is to say, it is a factor that makes some animals fit and others less fit. Finally, what precisely do we mean by a 'species'? We say that two animals are of different species if they are normally prevented from breeding together and producing fertile young of both sexes. Biologists will realize that this definition leaks a bit around the edges (what about asexually reproducing organisms, for example?), but it is good enough for this book. It means that the species is the range of gene exchange, and hence the field within which evolution can operate. If one cat's genes undergo a change (what we call a 'mutation'), and this produces a new, advantageous pattern of behaviour in that cat's offspring, then in principle evolutionary processes can spread that new behaviour to all the cats of some generation to come. There is no evolutionary way in which the new behaviour can appear in dogs.

Misunderstandings about evolution

There are several ways in which people thinking about behaviour sometimes misunderstand evolutionary theory. The most basic error is to suppose that evolution will always produce the best possible solution to any environmental problem – in the terms just

6

introduced, that organisms will always be ideally adapted to their ecological niches. This is a mistake in several different ways.

There are, in fact, sound reasons why evolution is unlikely to produce the best possible solution. Chief among them is the fact that it is a historical process. It may not be possible to reach the best possible solution from the point at which an evolutionary process happens to start. The historical nature of the evolutionary process has been strongly emphasized by Gould and Lewontin (1979), who argue that two species may reach quite different, equally good, solutions to similar problems because they took different evolutionary routes; and that this makes interpretations of species differences in terms of adaptiveness extremely hazardous.

Also, by the 'best possible solution', people often mean what is best for the species as a whole. But evolution does not take place by competition between one species and another. It takes place by competition between one individual and another (or, more precisely, one gene and another) within a species. What evolves will therefore be what is good for individuals, not what is good for the species. This is a central theme of the most recent biological approach to behaviour, known as *sociobiology*. Earlier authors were not always too clear on it. We shall return to this point many times in the course of this book.

A second misconception about evolution is to suppose that, because the word 'evolution' implies gradual change (it is often opposed to 'revolution'), evolutionary change is going on at a more or less constant rate, with new species being produced at roughly the same low frequency throughout the history of life. But this is not what happens at all. Instead, one species of animals makes a crucial advance, and a great range of species promptly differentiate from it to fill a great number of niches, probably displacing earlier species in the process. Evolution of new species further alters the environment for other unrelated species, and so applies new selective pressures which may trigger off yet more rapid differentiation. Evolutionary biologists think of the history of life as consisting of a series of 'punctuated equilibria', with long periods during which relatively few new species appear followed by 'adaptive radiations' as entire new groups evolve. The fossil record supports this picture.

One final misconception must be nailed before we proceed to

look at some criticisms of evolutionary theory. To produce an evolutionary explanation of any behavioural phenomenon is to show that it is 'natural'. That is what the word natural means, if it means anything at all when applied to behaviour. All too often, people will proceed to draw the conclusion that because some kind of behaviour is natural, it must also be morally justifiable or even to be positively sought after, and in any case that it will inevitably occur. In the course of this book, we shall find that it may be natural for men to kill their stepchildren, women to be unfaithful to loyal husbands, children to rob their siblings. Neither I nor any evolutionary biologist is saying that these things are desirable, justifiable or inevitable; simply that they are tendencies that exist in people. Some critics have understood that much, but seem to believe that if such tendencies are natural, the less said about the fact the better. This too is untenable. Unpalatable truths are better faced; then it becomes possible to do something about them. It is scarcely a new idea to western thought that human beings have some deplorable behavioural tendencies, for if we did not we should have no need of moral principles.

Criticisms of evolutionary theory

Although evolution is the central idea in modern biology, that does not mean that it is, or should be, above criticism. The almost religious attachment of some biologists to evolution is inappropriate, for it is conceivable that Darwin's theory could one day be replaced by something else. Even now, in some obscure laboratory, a palaeontologist could be piecing together conclusive evidence that all living species were created a few thousand years ago by genetic engineers from Mars, who then hopped into their flying saucers and flew away, pausing only to scatter a few misleading fossils. Don't laugh: it's a logical possibility. Any scientific theory can always be superseded.

The commonest criticism of evolutionary theory in fact argues that it is losing this provisional quality, which always characterizes scientific ideas, and is becoming a sort of super-flexible dogma, into which any facts whatsoever can be fitted.

This objection must always be borne in mind, as a warning against what we can call 'armchair adaptationism' – thinking up evolutionary explanations for behaviour without considering how they could ever be checked against data. This does indeed lead to a pseudo-science of no interest. The sophisticated way of putting this kind of objection is to appeal to the ideas of Sir Karl Popper (1959) and argue that evolutionary theory cannot be scientific because it is not falsifiable – there is no conceivable set of observations that could show it to be wrong. The Popperian critic of an evolutionary approach to behaviour would say that there is no behaviour for which we could not think up an evolutionary explanation. Once again, this is true if, but only if, we let ourselves slide into armchair adaptationism. What we have to do is guard, jealously, the *empirical content* of our theorizing – the extent to which it says something about the real world that is open to an empirical test, that is to being examined by observation and experiment rather than just by logical analysis.

A second kind of criticism focuses either on the idea of gradual change implicit in the word 'evolution', or on the phrase 'natural selection', with its implication that particular, fit individuals (usually the best-adapted ones) will spread their characteristics to succeeding generations. From time to time one hears reports of evidence that species may have developed from each other by sudden jumps, or by purely random changes in the 'gene pool' (the stock of genes represented in the population), and that speciation by either of these routes casts doubt on Darwin's theories. Both these processes are in fact predicted by modern evolutionary theory – they are known as 'saltation' and 'genetic drift' respectively, and both are known to occur. All genetic change must have at least some random component, and we have already seen that new species do not emerge at a constant rate from millennium to millennium. There is room for argument about the quantitative importance of genetic drift and the size of the genetic 'jumps' that make the important contributions to evolution. But the most fervent supporters of drift and saltation do not see themselves as setting up an alternative to Darwinism; on the contrary, some of them claim to be returning to the true spirit of Darwin in the face of armchair adaptationism elsewhere in the scientific community. For in the phenomena of saltation and drift we certainly do have another warning against the armchair as a research tool. A good way of looking foolish would be to spend time thinking up ingenious adaptationist explanations for the evolution of the modern wheat plant, for example, when, given the chromosomal make-up of wheat and its near relatives, their evolution must have involved a very small number of sudden cross-breedings (McFadden and Sears, 1947).

A third kind of criticism of evolutionary theory is the theological. Notoriously, Darwin and his followers were involved in heated disputes with churchmen and theologians, and there can be no doubt that the idea of natural selection and the idea of a purposive and omnipotent creator are uncomfortable bedfellows. Darwin's own religious beliefs soon fell victim to this conflict, as he relates in his autobiography (Darwin, 1887/1958, pp. 85–96). It would not be proper for this book to enter into theological disputes, though it may be worth pointing out that there has never been any shortage of evolutionary biologists (from contemporaries of Darwin's like Charles Kingsley down to the present author) who have counted themselves Christians; and that such 'Christian Darwinians' have tended to be theologically orthodox (Moore, 1979). There is a sense in which scientific and theological ideas can never really come into collision, because they are different orders of statement: scientific beliefs are always provisional, while religions claim to state eternal truths. But those who believe in the literal truth of every word of the Bible have always felt themselves in conflict with evolutionary theory, and probably always will. Even this conflict can be resolved, however, as the nineteenth-century biologist and fundamentalist P.H. Gosse realized: he proposed that God must have created the world exactly as if it had been evolving over a much longer time scale than Scripture allows. Even Adam, Gosse (1857) argued, must have had a navel. For some reason this logically unassailable position is always treated with derision.

The criticisms we have considered so far apply to the theory of evolution as a whole. Two others are particularly concerned with evolutionary accounts of behaviour. Both come from outside biology. The first is aimed at the sociobiologists, who lay particular stress on the role of competition in creating selective pressures. Their critics point out that this kind of evolutionary theory has certain resemblances to the theory of the free market economy, and they therefore suggest that an evolutionary approach to behaviour is the product of a capitalist society, put forward not because it is supported by data, but in a conscious or unconscious attempt to provide a justification for that kind of social organization. There certainly are parallels between evolutionary theory and market economics, as several economists have recently pointed out (e.g. Guha, 1981; Hirshleifer, 1977). Competition is indeed at the heart of both. There have been social philosophers who have taken Darwinism as justification for allowing the survival of the fittest to be the rule of human government. But there is no logic in doing so. Even if competition between firms could be said to be a product of evolution, and therefore 'natural', it would not for that reason be either morally right or socially efficient, and no modern evolutionary biologist would fall into the fallacy of supposing that it was. An evolutionary approach to behaviour cannot be represented as justifying capitalism red in tooth and claw. As to whether it is the product of minds infected with capitalism, readers must judge for themselves how well the evolutionary account of behaviour presented in this book fits the available data – provided, of course, that their own minds are not so diseased by capitalism that their judgement is hopelessly biased!

Finally, we have a critique which applies particularly to evolutionary accounts of human behaviour. Evolution depends on the passing on of characteristics from one generation to another by genes. Yet, with the coming of human language, we have a different way in which one generation may influence the next. You and I share the ability to learn a language. No doubt that is something we inherited from our parents through our genes, and we owe it to natural selection. But the English language, which we also share, and which we also inherited from our parents, was passed on to us by non-genetic means, and we owe it to a quite different sort of evolution, studied by philologists, not biologists. It is part of our culture, not of our biology. For many human behaviours, it is a very real and open question whether they are passed on by genetic or cultural means. Why do most societies have strong prohibitions against sexual activities between brothers and sisters, or mothers and sons? It is easy to see why such a tendency should be carried in our genes, but equally easy to see how it could be perpetuated by cultural processes. The debate here is not about whether evolutionary theory is correct, but about the limits of its proper application. This is a lively current controversy, and we shall meet it at many points in this book. One of the most interesting recent developments is an increasing acceptance by evolutionary biologists of the importance of culture

– but with the assertion that cultural traits will be subject to selective pressures rather like those affecting genes. The theory of 'cultural evolution' is now developing rapidly – or, should one say, evolving.

The limits of evolutionary explanation

Evolutionary explanations are only explanations in a limited sense. They provide answers to the 'Why?' questions about behaviour – they explain it in terms of its *function*. But we also have 'How?' questions about behaviour, which need answers in terms of *mechanism*, the immediate factors in the life of the individual organism which cause the behaviour to occur. For example, baby cuckoos push their foster siblings out of the nest. We can provide a functional explanation of that behaviour by suggesting that it ensures the cuckoo a better food supply. But we also need a mechanistic explanation, in terms of the precise stimuli from the other nestlings that induce the cuckoo to start throwing them out, the precise movements it makes in doing so, and so forth. Often we refer to this as a 'proximate' explanation, in contrast to the 'ultimate' explanation offered by evolution. For any behaviour of any complexity, we also need a third kind of account, a 'developmental' explanation, which will centre on the way the behaviour emerges and is perfected within the life span of the individual. Evolutionary explanations cannot tell the whole story.

This is only a short book, and it cannot give equal weight to all these aspects of behaviour. I have chosen to say rather little about the development of behaviour, rather more about its mechanisms, and a lot about its function. None of the three kinds of explanation can be ignored, though. As we turn now from setting the scene for a biological explanation of behaviour to describing the characters who have played in it, we shall find that all of them have given at least some attention to all three aspects of the biology of behaviour.

Comparative ethology: how biologists study the behaviour of individuals

The actors on the ethological stage are, of course, the ethologists. There is more than one kind of ethologist, and it is important to grasp the differences between them, because they tend to study different kinds of behaviour, and to use the theory of evolution in different ways. Also, they do not always agree with one another. The first group I shall introduce is the oldest and best known. It was they who formulated the idea of a distinct branch of zoology specifically concerned with behaviour and began to call themselves ethologists. The best-known figures in this group are Konrad Lorenz and Niko Tinbergen. Of course, biologists have always been interested in behaviour. Behavioural observations played their part in the formation of Darwin's ideas, as is immediately obvious when you read the *Origin of Species* or *The Descent of Man*. Lorenz and Tinbergen recognized an earlier generation (Wallace Craig, Oskar Heinroth, Julian Huxley, Charles Whitman) as the 'fathers of ethology', and some of the ideas to be presented in this book were expressed by these early-twentieth-century authors. But it is in the work of Lorenz, Tinbergen and their colleagues in continental Europe that they are first brought together and formulated clearly.

These early ethologists made explicit the idea that behaviour could be studied in just the same way as any other aspect of life. Different species of animals have different skeletons; they also have different behaviour. The skeletons of animals that lie within related groups (for example, the skeletons of all ducks and geese) tend to be similar; the behaviour of all ducks and geese is also similar. The differences between different animals' skeletons can be related to the differences in the environments they live in, the food they eat and the predators they have to avoid; the differences in different animals' behaviour can be related to exactly the same ecological pressures. The skeleton of any individual animal develops in an orderly way from the moment of fertilization through to adulthood; the development of behaviour is also orderly and open to study. This series of claims, self-evident once stated, was virtually a manifesto for the early ethologists.

Crook (1970) has suggested that we should label this approach to the study of behaviour 'comparative ethology', to distinguish it from a rather different way of going about things, to be considered in the next section of this chapter. Comparative ethology is still a lively research tradition, and its findings not only occupy almost the whole of chapters 2 and 3 of this book but continue to crop up right to the end. It is one indispensable part of the biological approach to behaviour, but it is no longer the only way of making such an approach.

Social ethology: how biologists study societies

Crook argued that, apart from comparative ethology, there was another way of studying behaviour as a part of biology. He called this 'social ethology'. Whereas comparative ethologists study the behaviour of individual animals towards each other, and try to build up a picture of animal society from those, social ethologists, according to Crook, start from the society, consider that as a biological entity in itself, and then try to understand individual behaviours in terms of their relation to the entire society. Social ethology, Crook argued, was relatively under-developed. In particular, in relating behaviour to evolution, comparative ethology had paid too little attention to the *social* environment; Crook argued that the most important selection pressures operating on a social animal would be those generated within the society.

Crook's paper, published in 1970, comes closer than anything else I know in scientific writing to an act of clairvoyance. In 1975 E.O. Wilson published a massive reference text entitled *Sociobiology*; a year later Richard Dawkins produced a magnificently readable introduction to the same material, *The Selfish Gene*. Suddenly, the study of animal behaviour was transformed. At a conference in 1977, Dawkins said 'Revolution is in the air'. He was not exaggerating. The kind of scientific revolution described by the historian of science T.S. Kuhn (1962) was in full swing.

As in all scientific revolutions, the change in scientists' perceptions was more sudden than the change in what they were doing. Interest in social ethology had been growing for at least the previous decade. But quite suddenly, almost everyone perceived that they had been studying social ethology. They were also presented with a theoretical system to apply in their research. That system has come to be known as 'sociobiology'.

Wilson set out the basic claim of sociobiology as being entirely parallel to the basic claim of the early ethologists. Just as Lorenz and Tinbergen stressed that behaviour could be treated as a biological entity, like any other aspect of life, so Wilson claimed that animal societies could be treated as biological entities. That is to say, societies are to be understood in terms of evolution by natural selection. Societies are larger units than individuals, of course, and so the methods of treating their behaviour biologically are rather different; whereas Lorenz and other comparative ethologists thought of themselves as being in a sense physiologists of behaviour, Wilson's reference areas in biology were population biology and ecology.

Wilson's ideas have proved highly controversial. In this book, I try to maintain a careful distinction between social ethology, which is a field of study, and sociobiology, which is a theoretical system applied to that field of study. It is possible to be interested in social ethology without being a sociobiologist. None the less, the basic method of the sociobiologists permeates this book. That basic method is to ask, of every behaviour, what would be the evolutionary fate of a gene that produced that behaviour, given the environment in which the organism bearing that gene must live. This sounds simple enough, though it obviously demands some knowledge of both genetics and ecology. But there is a crucial twist. As Crook pointed out, for social animals the most important aspect of the environment is the other members of the social group. They, too, will be bearing the gene we are interested in, or alternative genes that are competing with it over the evolutionary time scale. This makes working out the likely success of any given gene a far from simple matter.

Behavioural ecology

Yet another group of biologists are interested in behaviour. The sociobiology revolution has had the effect of bringing ecological questions to the attention of everyone interested in behaviour, but long before that happened there were ecologists who were particularly interested in how behaviour contributed to an animal's equilibrium with its environment.

Some of the concerns of these 'behavioural ecologists' were very close to those of the sociobiologists. Take territory as an example. It is well known that certain species of animals tend to establish small areas of land (or water) which they defend, driving off all other members of their own species except, in some cases, their mate and offspring. This interests sociobiologists because it is one extreme kind of social structure, but it also interests behavioural ecologists, because a territorial animal gives itself exclusive access to a particular quantity of resources. An ecologist will be interested in the worth to the animal of those resources, and also in the cost of defending them (in terms of time and energy expenditure). Other concerns of behavioural ecology fit less well into sociobiology but none the less form an important part of a comprehensive study of the biology of behaviour. An example is foraging theory, which is concerned with the means animals use to collect prey (animal or vegetable) from the environment. Foraging may have little to do with social behaviour. On the other hand, it does raise questions which have been discussed in the past by psychologists studying animal learning using food reward. In recent years the ecological and psychological approaches have been drawing closer together, with traditional animal psychology tending to become more integrated into a broadly based biological treatment of behaviour. These developments are discussed further in chapter 6.

The key questions for this book

We have set the scene and introduced the characters. All that we need now is a synopsis of the plot. The general aim of this book is to consider what all the different kinds of biological approach to behaviour can contribute to our understanding of ourselves. I have already said that we need to be severely sceptical about applying the results of ethology directly to human affairs. This book is not going to explain your behaviour by whipping a few grey-lag geese out of a hat. What specific questions can we hope to answer?

The next chapter tries to explain what we nowadays mean by 'instinct'. No evolutionary account of behaviour could possibly work unless behavioural tendencies can be inherited genetically, and simple instincts are the surest instances of inherited behaviours that we have. The following two chapters explain first how instincts, and then how societies as a whole, are moulded by evolution. Next, I give an account, based on both comparative ethology and sociobiology, of the main social relationships, between males and females and between parents and young. Finally come two chapters in which I consider how all of this is modified by the facts that animals are able to learn, and so are not mere creatures of instinct, and that humans are able to learn language, and so become caught up in cultural evolution as well as genetic evolution.

Through all this, I am seeking answers to two more basic questions. First, how good an account of animal behaviour can we give in terms of evolution? Secondly, how do humans fit in with or deviate from the pattern established for other animals? In other words, granted that our species is a special case, exactly what sort of special case are we? We know that we were produced by evolution. Have we completely outgrown our ancestry? Or are we still bound by laws that also govern our fellow animals?

2

Instinct

The word 'instinct' is one that we often use in everyday life. 'The child ran in front of my car, and instinctively I slammed on the brakes.' 'Mothers know by instinct what is best for their children.' 'There's nothing so powerful as the mating instinct.'

These examples are all rather different, but they have one point in common. We talk about actions as 'instinctive' when they are done without conscious planning. Scientists use the word in the same way, as the opposite of 'intelligent' or 'reasoned'. But in scientific usage, 'instinctive' carries two extra meanings. One of them is helpful, the other is not.

First, to a scientist, 'instinctive' generally implies 'innate' or 'inborn' – the opposite of 'learned' rather than the opposite of 'reasoned'. By extension, 'instinct' is often used to refer to broad behavioural tendencies, which are widely believed to be innate: we talk about 'the mating instinct', 'the maternal instinct', 'the gregarious instinct', and so forth. In other contexts we might call these 'drives' or 'motivations'.

This specialized scientific meaning of 'instinct' is quite reasonable. What is not reasonable, however, is the tendency to see the *description* of behaviour as instinctive as in some way an *explanation*. This is obviously wrong. To say that some behaviour takes place without conscious calculation, or even without individual learning, is in no way to explain it; it is simply to label it as being, so far, unexplained. Scientists working on behaviour were quick to spot this problem. Psychologists such as William McDougall (e.g. 1932), who had made much use of the concept of instinct, fell out of fashion. In mainstream British and American psychology, in fact, the very use of the word 'instinct' came to be taken as a sign of sloppy or outdated thinking. It was against this background that the Dutch ethologist, Niko Tinbergen, published in 1951 a book entitled *The Study of Instinct*.

Why do greylag geese roll eggs with their beaks?

Tinbergen's book gave the English-speaking world an account of the continental ethologists' methods, results and conclusions in the study of animal behaviour. To see how and why this revolutionized our approach to instinct we shall look at just one of the pieces of behaviour Tinbergen described.

Lorenz and Tinbergen (1938/1970) made an intensive study of the behaviour of greylag geese in more or less natural situations. They noticed a very odd thing. Whenever a sitting goose lost an egg from her nest, she always retrieved it in the same way. She would turn to face the egg, stretch out her neck, walk slowly towards the egg, hook her beak over it and roll it slowly back into the nest. This did not seem to be particularly efficient: sometimes it took several attempts before the egg was safely back in the nest; sometimes the goose never succeeded in getting it back. But never did she sweep the egg back underneath her with her wing or kick the egg back in with her feet.

Why not? Why should greylag geese retrieve eggs with their beaks? Lorenz and Tinbergen started to answer this question by labelling egg-rolling as 'instinctive'. They meant by this that the goose had not consciously decided to recover her egg in that way. They also meant that the goose had not learned by trial and error that rolling with the beak was the best method of egg-recovery. But Lorenz and Tinbergen knew that this was in no way an explanation. To call egg-rolling instinctive was, to them, simply a way of saying that the answer to 'Why do greylag geese roll eggs with their beaks?' is 'Because they are greylag geese'! And that is clearly not an answer at all.

The comparative method in ethology

But it points the way to an answer, because it prompts a further question: 'What, then, *is* a greylag goose?' Tinbergen, Lorenz and their colleagues had been trained as zoologists. So far as they were concerned, to ask 'What is' a particular animal was to ask where it fitted in to the great scheme of relationships and groupings between different kinds of living things that was first proposed by Linnaeus in the eighteenth century, and given sense and theoretical explanation by Darwin's theory of evolution a hundred years later. What a greylag goose is, from this point of view, is first and foremost a goose, related more or less closely to other species of geese, such as Emperor geese or Canada geese, and more or less distantly to all the many species of ducks; more distantly still to other kinds of birds, then to other vertebrates and so forth. Lorenz looked at the various behaviours of all sorts of geese and ducks. He found that some geese and ducks showed the same or closely similar behaviours, while others did not. Broadly speaking, the more closely two species are related, the more likely they are to share any particular kind of behaviour.

This sort of comparison of the behaviours of species, whose relationship is known, is the hallmark of the comparative method in ethology. In our struggle to get to grips with the slippery concept of instinct, it does two things for us. First, as we have just seen, it provides an answer to the question 'What is a greylag goose?' (or a herring gull, or a stickleback, or a European robin, or whatever): it fits each species into a pattern of related species. Secondly, it provides evidence in favour of egg-rolling (or whatever the behaviour under consideration is) being innate. If the same behaviour is shown in a number of other species that are believed to share common ancestors with the greylag goose, and not found in less closely related species, it seems very probable that the behaviour in question has come down to the greylag by descent.

This comparative method will obviously work only if we can find behaviours that are very nearly as stereotyped and durable as bones, teeth and the other structural properties of animals that are normally used by biologists who work out evolutionary relationships (such biologists are called 'comparative morphologists'). The early ethologists showed that such stereotyped behaviour patterns do exist. Nowadays, we call them 'fixed action patterns'.

Fixed action patterns

Ideally, a pattern of behaviour should have all the following characteristics if it is to be described as a fixed action pattern (the list is based on one offered by Lorenz, 1932/1970a, which I have expanded somewhat in the light of modern usage).

1 *Stereotypy:* the behaviour always occurs in the same form. This is one of those principles that needs taking with a grain of salt. No two occurrences of even so simple a behaviour as egg-rolling are going to be completely identical. But stereotypy is important for all that: it would be impossible to apply the comparative method to behaviours that changed out of all recognition from one occurrence to the next.

2 *Universality:* the behaviour occurs in all members of a species. This, too, needs qualification; if a single animal's behaviour patterns are not likely to be repeated exactly from one occurrence to the next, how much less likely are they to be just the same as another animal's performances? But this is really what is meant by universality: the variation between individuals should not be huge compared with the variations within an individual, from one trial to the next. Another qualification needs to be added to universality, though. It is only all members of a species *within defined classes* that should be expected to show the behaviour in question. We should not expect ganders or goslings, or even mother geese outside the nesting season, to show the egg-rolling behaviour. But we do expect all mother geese with nests to show it.

3 *Independence of individual experience:* fixed action patterns should occur regardless of the individual animal's past history. This leads directly to the ethologists' famous isolation experiment: an animal is reared by hand in isolation from all other members of its species. If you do this with a greylag goose, and then subsequently allow her to mate and lay eggs, her egg-rolling response will not be one whit different from that of any other goose. Hence she cannot have learned how to roll eggs from her

mother, her sisters or any other goose. The response must, argues Lorenz, deserve the term 'instinctive'. That is not to say that it is incapable of modification by experience: geese that participated in some of Lorenz and Tinbergen's experiments on egg-rolling soon became both more discriminating and more skilful in their behaviour. But on first emergence a fixed action pattern should occur in the same way in an isolation-reared animal as in a normal control.

4 *Ballisticness:* a ballistic response is one that cannot be varied if circumstances change after the response has been launched. Lorenz and Tinbergen illustrated this for the greylag goose's egg-rolling by offering a goose a giant egg, in fact a cardboard Easter egg painted with the same sort of markings as a real goose egg. The goose responded to this giant egg as though it was a real egg, and when it was put down just outside the goose's nest, she stretched out her neck, stepped towards the Easter egg, hooked her beak over it and began to roll it in. But of course she could not roll the giant egg underneath her, and it became stuck between her beak and her breast. At this point she might have moved her head to one side and swept the giant egg in with her wing, or something of that sort. In practice, however, she simply stayed as she was for some seconds and then stood up looking uncomfortable: she learned to avoid the Easter egg in future.

5 *Singleness of purpose:* fixed action patterns have only one function. Hooking an egg in with the beak is not the most efficient way of recovering an egg. But it is a method that works, and one imagines that it could be useful in other contexts, for example in nest-building, herding goslings or even perhaps in feeding on the surface of water. Yet Lorenz says that the behaviour pattern is never shown in any other context except that of errant eggs. Psychologists working with animals have sometimes tried to train them to perform what were probably fixed action patterns in order to get food rewards, with singular lack of success. Sara Shettleworth (1975) systematically observed fixed action patterns in golden hamsters, and then rewarded hamsters with food whenever they emitted one of six of the commonest fixed action patterns. Shettleworth found that three responses which had plausible 'natural' connections with feeding soon increased in frequency, but that three others (scratching with a hind leg, face-washing and marking the apparatus walls using a scent gland located on the

animal's flanks) seemed largely unaffected by reward. They were not 'available' as food-getting responses.

6 *The existence of known trigger stimuli:* we can find some stimulus, or set of stimuli, which will reliably trigger the response. This final characteristic of fixed action patterns is so important that it deserves a section to itself.

Sign stimuli

It is easy to confuse the function of a response with its cause. The function of the greylag goose's egg-rolling is to recover the egg. Egg-recovery is what the behaviour achieves. But egg-recovery is not the *cause* of the behaviour, for if we take an egg right away from the nest, we shall not see the goose stretching out her head and trying to drag in eggs that are not there. The cause of egg-rolling is the sight of an egg, or something that looks sufficiently like one, within reach from the nest. 'Looks sufficiently like one' turns out to be the key phrase here. Lorenz's experiment with the giant egg ought to warn us that what is and is not 'sufficiently like' may contain some surprises. It is just this power to surprise that gives us confidence that we are able to discover the causes of fixed action patterns.

To see this process of discovery at work, we can turn to another much studied fixed action pattern, the begging response of the herring-gull chick as studied by Tinbergen and his colleagues in the Netherlands. Herring gulls nest on the ground. The parents go off to feed at sea, on a local scrap heap or at some other distant source of food. When they return, they land on their small nesting territory and stand near (often over) the chick, pointing their beaks at the ground. The chick then pecks at the parent's beak, which stimulates the parent to regurgitate the food it has collected, allowing the chick to feed.

Because the parent gulls spend much of their time away from the nest, foraging, it is fairly easy to get close to the chicks and investigate whether the begging response can be produced by anything short of the apparent natural stimulus, the parent's head. Tinbergen and his colleagues tried a number of stimuli, including a life-like three-dimensional model of a gull's head, but they found that it did not take anything very elaborate to elicit begging: a simple cardboard cutout of a gull's head, with no more detail on it than an eye and a beak, was quite sufficient. Equipped with this basic pattern, Tinbergen and Perdeck (1950) set out to discover what features of the parent's head were important in stimulating begging. They tried a large number of variations with different chicks, and recorded how often they were able to elicit a response with each one. The adult herring gull has a white head, a yellow bill and a small red spot a third of the way from the end of the lower mandible. Tinbergen and Perdeck used three series of cardboard cutout heads. The first series tested the effect of spot colour: all the models had yellow beaks with spots on, but the spots were of different colours: unsurprisingly, the chicks pecked most at the 'head' with the red-spotted beak, though black, blue and white spots also elicited a good number of responses. The second series tested the effect of contrast between spot and beak. The models all had medium-grey bills, and the spot colour was varied from white through shades of grey to black. Here the middle-grey spots made for the least effective stimulus; the most effective were those with the black or white spots. The final series of heads tested the effect of bill colour, using models with no spots on their beaks. Here the results were more surprising. A yellow bill, the 'natural' colour, was not as effective as a red one, and in general the nearer the beak colour to red the more effective the stimulus.

Tinbergen and Perdeck's third series of artificial heads make an important point. The most effective stimulus for eliciting a fixed action pattern is not necessarily the one that is most like the normal stimulus. Tinbergen and Perdeck rammed this point home with another artificial stimulus. They tried the effect of a thin, pointed red rod with three white bands around its end. This turned out to be extremely effective: it was in fact 26 per cent more likely to elicit a response than the accurate, three-dimensional plaster model of the herring gull's head.

An artificial stimulus which is more effective than the 'real thing' in this way is referred to as a 'super-normal stimulus' or a 'super-releaser' (we shall see where the 'releaser' part of this comes from in a moment). Strictly speaking, of course, Tinbergen and Perdeck's thin red rod was not a proved super-releaser because they did not compare its effectiveness with the parent gull itself. An undeniable super-releaser effect is seen, however, in another experiment by Tinbergen (1948) using oystercatchers. The oystercatcher is that handsome black-and-white wading bird, with a red bill and a whistling cry, which can be seen around most British coasts. It nests on the ground, laying superbly camouflaged eggs in what is barely more than a scrape. The eggs of all ground-nesting seabirds tend to be rather similar, of course, because they are all adapted to be camouflaged in the same environment: a herring gull's egg thus looks very much like an oystercatcher's egg, but twice the size. Yet Tinbergen found that if he put a herring-gull egg near an oystercatcher nest, the returning oystercatcher would go and brood the outsize gull egg instead of its own. Worse, if he constructed an artificial egg so large that the oystercatcher could barely straddle it let alone sit on it, and painted it with a scaled-up version of the green-and-brown speckled pattern of an oystercatcher egg, the bird would choose this absurd giant egg instead of its own or the gull's egg. Here is an undeniable super-releaser.

The possibility of constructing such super-normal stimuli gives us confidence that we really can discover the key features of the stimuli that cause fixed action patterns. In the case of the herring-gull chick's begging response, these key features seem to be redness and contrast (to be exact, contour, that is places where light intensity changes). In the case of the brooding response of the oystercatcher, it seems to be speckliness and size – the bigger the speckles and the bigger the egg, the stronger the response. Such key features are referred to by ethologists as 'sign stimuli'.

Releasers

More often, however, you will hear the stimuli that trigger off fixed action patterns referred to as either 'releasers' or as 'releasing stimuli'. Lorenz (e.g. 1937/1970c) used both terms (sign stimulus and releaser), but he meant them to have slightly different meanings, and it is instructive to make the distinction clear: it will be important later in the book.

Consider two of the sign stimuli we have studied so far, the blotches on the oystercatcher's egg and the red spot on the herring gull's bill. Why does each of these features exist? As we saw in chapter 1, biologists always want to answer 'Why?' questions by appealing to natural selection. In general, therefore, we must answer that, presumably, oystercatchers that lay blotchy eggs leave more descendants than oystercatchers that don't; and herring gulls with red spots on their bills leave more descendants than herring gulls without them. But what is the likely origin of the selective advantage in each case?

In the case of the oystercatcher, the answer is surely camouflage. It is all too easy to walk within inches of an oyster-catcher nest and never know it is there. Presumably oystercatchers that lay blotchy eggs are less likely to be deprived of them by foxes, gulls, humans or other visually guided predators. There is no comparable explanation for the spot on the herring gull's bill. Its only obvious advantage is to provide something to elicit begging from the chick. Lorenz proposed that we should limit the term 'releaser' to cases like this, where a structure seems to have evolved for no other reason than that it is a sign stimulus. The blotches on the oystercatcher's egg are therefore not releasers: their function as sign stimuli is apparently secondary to their function in camouflage.

Most of the sign stimuli we shall study will be releasers in the strict sense, a fact that causes some people to forget the distinction between the two terms. But it is an important distinction, especially when we start to think about the adaptive advantage conferred by behaviours or structures related to them. It is all too easy to slip into armchair adaptationism, making up functions for structures, while forgetting that they may have evolved (or been exaggerated) because of their effects on other animals, of the same or different species; or to concentrate on 'signalling' effects, ignoring the possibility that the sign-stimulus effect of a structure may be parasitic on some more mundane function. Let me take a conten-tious example to illustrate the dangers. The human female breast undoubtedly has a straightforward function, in secreting and delivering milk. It also undoubtedly has an effect on other mem-bers of the human species, specifically on sexually active males, and many people would want to call this effect 'instinctive'. With a little knowledge of evolutionary theory, it is extremely tempting to produce either of two very shallow stories out of this. On the one hand, some people might suppose that large breasts are correlated with a good milk supply and therefore signal a good potential mother, and so this explains men's 'instinctive' interest in them: in so far as they elicit fixed action patterns, they do so as sign stimuli but not as releasers in the strict sense. Others might point out that the children of small-breasted mothers do not seem to starve, and so would argue that large breasts must have evolved as releasers, with the sole function of eliciting appropriate responses from males.

The point of the illustration is that neither of these arguments can be justified with the information available to the average lounge-bar pundit. There are ways of investigating what the functions of a putative releaser are. One is to use a comparative technique: for reasons that we shall explore in the next chapter, true releasers are quite often found in one species but not in other, closely related species, while structures with non-signalling functions are usually more 'evolutionarily conservative' unless they are related to something obviously unique about an animal's environment. In the case of the human breast, Desmond Morris (1967, p. 70) points out that the great apes manage to feed their young with almost no breast development except while actually lactating, which favours a 'releaser' account. Another way of investigating a releaser's function is to look at how reproductive success is correlated with natural variations in the structure in question: thus the fact that there is no obvious correlation between breast size and milk production also favours a releaser account. But clearly a great deal more evidence is needed before we can be sure. The whole question of evolutionary explanations of behaviour is taken up in detail in the next chapter: the point of these mammary asides has been to make clear that such explanations should not be offered too glibly or accepted too lightly.

Drive

Going on the examples we have considered so far, fixed action patterns seem to be biologically important pieces of behaviour. We have considered examples relating to feeding, parenting, mating and predator avoidance; we could have added instances relating to hunting, attacking other members of the same species, resisting attack or submitting to it, obtaining or defending territory, sleep and arousal. Some of these are behaviours which an animal may need to be ready to show at any time. A vole should be ready to avoid an owl, for example, no matter what the conditions (or should it? Readiness might be wasteful if the vole was safely in a burrow). Others are clearly appropriate only in certain circumstances. One much studied set of fixed action patterns, for example, involves the responses of male sticklebacks to females in mating condition. Clearly we would not expect even the most potent of males to react to even the most super-normal female during the winter, when it is too cold to rear young, or in late spring, when he already has a nest to look after. Or take the herring-gull chick again: it is a small animal, with a limited stomach capacity. Should it be prepared to beg when its parent has only just left (and, given that gulls typically forage far from their nest sites, is most unlikely to return very soon under natural conditions)? Clearly this would scarcely be adaptive.

In general, the probability that a fixed action pattern will be elicited is not a function of the presence or absence of sign stimuli alone. There are two other kinds of influence: the general external environment, and the internal environment. By the general external environment, we mean things like whether or not a vole is down its burrow; or what the temperature or day length is and how it is changing; or whether or not the animal is on its own home territory. For example, on his own territory, a male stickleback will respond to the releaser of another male stickleback's red throat by charging at the intruder and posturing in front of him; off his territory, he will respond to the same stimulus by fleeing.

By the internal environment, we mean the state of the animal's body, in practice often the state of its endocrine system – its hormones. Sometimes it is possible to demonstrate very dramatic effects of hormones on behaviour, and sometimes the hormones give us externally visible signs of their presence. As an example of both, consider singing in the male chaffinch. If you capture a cock chaffinch during the spring, and play him a recording of another cock chaffinch's song, he will (if he is appropriately housed) respond by singing himself. But keep the same cock chaffinch until autumn, and play him the same tape recording, and you will get no response. An injection of testosterone, the male sex hormone, will immediately restore his singing, however. Furthermore, the spring cock has a deep-blue-black bill, while the autumn cock's bill is pink: the testosterone injection gives the autumn cock a black bill as well as making him sing.

This is a case where we know how to produce a change in the

internal environment, how to monitor it and how it affects behaviour. More often, we do not know any of these things. What we
observe is that something in the outside world produces a change
in the probability that a sign stimulus will elicit a fixed action
pattern. For example, we observe that a stickleback on its territory
attacks red objects, while off its territory it flees from them; or we
observe that a herring-gull chick that has not eaten for thirty
minutes pecks at a cutout head model, while one that fed thirty
seconds ago does not. We are then tempted to take two steps,
neither of them really justifiable. First, we suppose that these
external conditions must produce some change in the internal
environment, which we could measure if we only knew how.
Secondly, we proceed to explain the change in the effect of the
stimulus in terms of this supposed change in the internal environment.

Why are these two steps illegitimate? In the first place, unless
we are to stretch the meaning of 'internal environment' unbearably, there is an alternative possibility. The change might be
registered only in the animal's brain: maybe the stickleback simply
'knows' that it is on, or off, its own territory, without any involve-
ment of hormones or anything of the sort. Perhaps it does not
matter too much if we think of such cognitive changes as involving
the internal environment, except that we may waste some time
looking for hormone changes that do not exist. The second step is
the really unsatisfactory one. We appeal to a change in the internal
environment to 'explain' the change in response to the sign
stimulus; but that change in response is our only evidence that the
internal environment has changed. This is a circular argument,
and it simply won't do.

The early ethologists did their best to avoid this elementary
logical (strictly, epistemological) blunder. They avoided speculations about the internal environment, and instead talked in terms
of motivational quantities which they called 'drives'. Thus they
proposed a hunger drive, a mating drive, an aggressive drive, a
parenting drive, and so forth. Most of these drives seemed to
Lorenz to have the property of building up over time unless
'released' – so that hunger is released by eating, aggression by
fighting, and so forth. Furthermore, Lorenz noticed that each of
the fixed action patterns which served these major drives seemed
to have its own deprivation properties. Leyhausen (1973) describes

29

this well for cats' hunting behaviour. A well-fed cat will not hunt much, of course (too little hunger drive, in Lorenz's terms). But in the presence of a glut of mice, a cat that has caught several mice without having to stalk them will start stalking distant mice without going on to pounce on them. The ethologists concluded that there were 'action specific energies' associated with each individual fixed action pattern.

Lorenz and Tinbergen were well aware that in itself 'drive' does not explain variations in response to a constant stimulus, any more than speculation about the internal environment does. Its sole merit is that it does not really *look* as if it is an explanation. It looks like what it is, a label for our ignorance. Unfortunately, psychologists have been less clear about this, and Lorenz's work became known among psychologists at a time when the comparative psychologist Clark Hull (e.g. 1952) had built up an elaborate systematic explanation of learning in which drive, introduced for exactly the reasons it was needed in ethology, played a prominent and explanatory part. So it is worth re-emphasizing that to talk about a hunger drive, or a sex drive, or an aggressive drive is not an explanation at all unless we are willing to say a whole lot more about what we mean by drive. Drives as such are no more than explanatory fictions: there is no evidence for their existence except the phenomena they are supposed to explain.

Seen through the eyes of a psychologist, Lorenz's system is what we call a 'connectionism'. The archetypal connectionist was E.L. Thorndike (e.g. 1913), who held that all behaviour could be understood in terms of the determination of stimuli by responses: if we could only specify what stimulus–response bonds were established within a person, or an animal, and specify the current stimuli, we should be able to predict behaviour perfectly. The scandal that haunts all connectionisms is motivation, for if motivation changes, the probabilities of all responses as a function of all stimuli will also change. All connectionisms have to be fudged in some way to deal with this, and the invention of drives is the classic means of fudging. There is nothing wrong with this in principle, if only because the alternative, non-connectionist ways of describing behaviour that are on offer are not all that impressive. The important point to understand is that drives are simply ways of talking about what connectionism cannot explain. They are not explanations for it.

The innate releasing mechanism

With the introduction of the drive concept, we can now complete Lorenz's account of instinctive behaviours. Lorenz proposed the simplest possible mechanism to account for what he had observed. He proposed that somewhere in the animal lies a centre, which he called the innate releasing mechanism (IRM). The various sign stimuli energize this mechanism, and so does drive. When it is sufficiently stimulated, the corresponding fixed action pattern occurs.

It has been said that the IRM is a perfectly useful concept so long as you remember that it is not innate, nor releasing, nor a mechanism: and there are indeed good grounds for being sceptical about all the three terms that appear in its name. But what we have to grasp now is that it is not an explanation of instinctive behaviours, but a description of them. As such it is clearly useful. If we specify that some aspect of an animal's behaviour fits the definition of a Lorenzian IRM, we know that we should look for sign stimuli, investigate what environmental variations will produce drive-like modulations of their releasing effect and look around for fixed action patterns. None of this explains anything. But what it does do is to produce a new and logically coherent definition of that vexed word 'instinct', with which we opened this chapter.

The point is that Lorenz, Tinbergen and many other ethologists since have documented large numbers of behavioural systems that do more or less fit Lorenz's description of an IRM. We have also found many other kinds of behaviour that do not fit that definition, but this does not matter so much. With the concept of an IRM firmly in mind, we have at least something against which we can compare newly discovered behaviour patterns. Fixed action patterns, sign stimuli, even drive effects are all objectively describable and recognizable. They come as close as we can get to being the behavioural analogues of bones and teeth that we need if we are to use the comparative method to good effect.

I shall refer to systems that can be described in terms of IRMs as 'micro-instincts'. This is to distinguish them from broad tendencies like hunger, sex and aggression, which we saw earlier are also sometimes described as instincts. Lorenz and Tinbergen both considered the question of how micro-instincts get integrated into larger behavioural units, and that question will be taken up in the next chapter.

Human instincts

All of this chapter has been concerned with animals, mainly birds and fish. In evolutionary terms, these are hundreds of millions of years separated from us, and it is easy to suppose that none of this material about micro-instincts has any relevance to human behaviour. Are not humans the creatures *par excellence* of reasoned response rather than reflex reaction, of intelligence rather than instinct?

The way this chapter began was meant, in part, as a warning against so simple an assertion. As a word, 'instinct' started life in the description of human affairs. Of course, we do not use the word in everyday speech with any idea of its technical, Lorenzian sense: but it is certainly not unreasonable to ask whether we humans have any micro-instincts in this sense.

The answer is that we almost certainly do. The best-established examples (and the easiest for most people to accept) concern the behaviour of very young infants. A brush on the cheek is supposed to make a hungry baby reflexively turn towards the touch, so helping it find the nipple, the most likely source of the stimulus. Prechtl (1958) studied this system and found that it had all the characteristics of a Lorenzian IRM. As the father of four breast-fed children, though, I have to say that according to my observations, if the survival of human infants depended on this IRM, my stock at least would be heading for extinction at a considerable rate.

There are systems that look very like IRMs in adults. Eibl-Eibesfeldt (1975) has studied the 'eyebrow-flash' response, shown in friendly greeting of someone you know: your eyebrows go up and your eyes open wide. Eibl-Eibesfeldt presents photographs of people from different racial and cultural groups all performing this response, and its form does seem to be remarkably constant. It is 'instinctive' in the everyday sense, too, in that it is something we do without being particularly aware of doing it and without particularly intending to.

More contentious but perhaps more significant examples can be found. We are inclined to smile at the oystercatcher, perched hopelessly on its barren giant egg, while its own egg lies neglected a few inches away. This seems to be the epitome of automatic, unintelligent behaviour, the kind of thing that the human species specializes in not doing. But which of us men has not given a second glance to an anatomically impossible picture of a woman, busting out of some advertisement? Or which of us, men or women, has not clucked gently over some winsomely presented baby, objectively too baby-faced to be real, but looking quite excessively charming? The features that an artist (or a photographer; the camera is an accomplished liar) exaggerates to produce a super-glamorous female form do not need scientific investigation. The features of a baby's face that elicit what one might call gooing behaviour from adults have recently been studied by Hall Sternglantz, Gray and Murakami (1977). They asked people to rate Identikit babies' faces for attractiveness, and showed that a high forehead, small chin and large eyes are critical (advertisers and cartoonists have obviously always known this). Hall Sternglantz and her colleagues also found that a face that possessed these features to a higher degree than any real baby was preferred to more realistic faces.

Here we have something that closely fits the definition of a super-releaser. The difference about human behaviour, perhaps, is that men do not leave their wives to ogle cartoon dollies, and human mothers do not abandon their own babies and offer to suckle the super-baby that appears in the women's magazine advertisement. But it is hubris to think that we are therefore so very superior to the oystercatcher. Even in humans, the preliminary, hormonal phases of response, at least, occur in response to artificial stimuli. Psychologists commonly use penile response to measure the erotic effects of pictures or even text (e.g. Geer and Fuhr, 1976). Clearly we are not immune to instincts, and just because instinctive responses may occur without thought or intention, even perhaps against our will, it is important to know what they are like. This chapter has attempted to describe them. The next chapter considers their origins.

3

The evolution of instincts

Lorenz's notion of the innate releasing mechanism made instinct a scientifically respectable concept, by giving us something coherent and recognizable we could talk about as an 'instinct'. But, as I stressed in the previous chapter, it was no accident that Lorenz and Tinbergen concentrated on these micro-behavioural systems. For the kind of analysis of behaviour which they, as zoologists, wanted, they needed something as clearly defined and recognizable as the bones and teeth used by morphologists. The IRM gave them what they needed. Armed with it, they could proceed to consider behaviour from an evolutionary perspective.

Despite its central role in biology, the theory of evolution is all too easy to abuse. The danger is to slip into armchair adaptationism. How can we avoid it? For the most part, the early ethologists concentrated on two ways of making out a rigorous evolutionary argument. First, they laid great stress on the comparative method, which we encountered in chapter 2. They recorded IRMs from large numbers of different but related species, so that they could compare the correlations between the IRMs of different species with the species' evolutionary relationships, as established from morphological and palaeontological (fossil) data. Secondly, they proposed a general mechanism by which IRMs could evolve. This second step was of great importance and considerable originality, and much of this chapter is devoted to it. In order to introduce it, we shall have to take a short detour, and consider what happens when an animal is acted upon by more than one drive.

Conflict of drives

If an animal has not eaten recently, certain fixed action patterns are likely to be elicited by the sight of food: we say that the animal is being acted upon by a hunger drive. If the animal is not in a place of absolute safety, certain other fixed action patterns are likely to be elicited by startling or biologically threatening stimuli: we say that the animal is acted upon by a fear drive. But what will happen when both food and threat are at the same place? Both drives will be active, but they will be tending to cause diametrically opposite kinds of behaviour.

This is what seems to happen with many animals if we put a new object down near their accustomed food source. The unfamiliar object is too frightening for the animal to come right up close to it and feed; but at a small distance it is much less threatening, while the chance of food remains highly attractive. The result is that the animal vacillates for quite some time a little way away from the object, until the conflict of drives is resolved either by the animal going away (presumably in search of a safer food source) or overcoming its fear and coming to feed.

There are two other very common sources of approach–avoid conflicts. One involves aggression. A rival animal of the same species may be, objectively, a threat to an animal: it may be likely to take away either food or mates. Not surprisingly, therefore, many animals are equipped with the means of fighting off other members of their species. But once this is true, a rival is an ambiguous stimulus. On the one hand, he or she should be approached and attacked. On the other hand, he or she is also capable of delivering an attack, and so should be avoided. Aggressive and fear drives come into conflict.

The other common approach–avoid conflict involves mating in what are called 'distance species'. The Swiss zoologist Hediger noticed that animals differ in how close to them they will let other members of their own species come. Some species, like rats, seals (and, oddly enough, hedgehogs and porcupines), are what Hediger called 'contact' species: if you keep several together in a cage, you will usually find them bundled up together in one large heap. Other species show what Hediger (1951) called 'individual distance': they are always found neatly spaced out, with no less than a certain fixed distance between each pair of neighbours. Most of the common garden birds have an individual distance. Gulls also show the phenomenon very nicely: it is common to see a group of gulls perched on the ridge of a roof, or a breakwater, neatly spaced out so that there are about 3 bird-widths between each bird and the next.

The concept of individual distance is one of those that social psychology has borrowed from ethology (though psychologists usually call it 'personal space'). It is certainly true that you can make someone acutely uncomfortable by violating their personal space, i.e. by standing inappropriately close to them. But it is doubtful whether human beings really meet the strict definition of a distance species. In the first place, we do not feel uncomfortable if even strangers come close to us when there is clearly a good cause, as in a crowded lift or train. In the second place, within families, personal space is effectively abolished. Parents and children, and lovers, tend to be constantly near to and touching each other, and in general this has nothing to do with parents providing care for children, or lovers preparing for copulation: it is simply a way of maintaining the relationships between people.

The situation for animals of a true distance species is quite different. The pair of blue tits that use the nesting box in my garden never seem to touch each other – except, presumably, for the act of copulation. For such animals, copulation involves a major conflict between whatever drive (fear?) keeps the two animals apart, and the sex drive which is compelling them to come together.

Displacement reactions

When we look at how animals behave in drive–conflict situations, we are faced with an unexpected result. It is very common to find that, when neither of the two conflicting response tendencies can be expressed in behaviour, some third kind of behaviour is shown. For example, two cocks facing each other, ready for a fight but each in conflict between attacking and running away, may suddenly break off and start to pull up grass. A cock zebra finch, in conflict between approaching a hen and flying away from her, may start to wipe his beak vigorously on the perch (Morris, 1959). A hungry rat put in an unfamiliar cage with food present may start to wash violently. These third responses, which emerge when two dominant responses are held in check by a drive conflict, are called 'displacement reactions'. Very often they involve preening, washing or other activities to do with the care of the body surface, but this may be simply because these are behaviours that are readily available. Nest-building, feeding and sleeping all occur as displacement responses too.

Many people have felt that the concept of displacement reactions can be applied to human behaviour. We are all familiar with the tendency to pace up and down, fiddle with any available object, smooth our hair, perhaps chew gum, nibble at cocktail snacks or smoke a cigarette, when we are uncertain what to do, or in a situation which makes us nervous but which we have to see through. Indeed, some situations are cartoon stereotypes for such behaviour: the nervous teenager on his first date, the prospective father in the waiting-room at the maternity hospital, and so forth. It is interesting that a number of the behaviours we think of as characteristic of such situations also come under the heading of 'care of the body surface': chewing nails, adjusting make-up, twirling a moustache, scratching your head, even (stretching the meaning of 'body surface' a little, but surely not unbearably) straightening a tie or smoothing a skirt.

This seems to me to be one of the more plausible analogies that can be drawn between ethological data and human behaviour. Also, the human case points up an important aspect of displacement responding. If we see a young man 'nervously' smoking cigarette after cigarette, we are able to use that observation to draw conclusions about his motivational state: we are apt to look around to find out what conflict of drives he is involved in. We are especially likely to do this if we are in some way a party to the conflict – if, say, we are the young woman he is trying to chat up.

Similarly, the displacement responses of animals may give other parties to the conflict information about the animal's drive state.

This fact is crucial to Lorenz's theory of the evolution of IRMs. Obviously it can only arise when the conflict involves more than one animal. The drives involved are therefore normally aggression, fear or sex.

Ritualization and emancipation of fixed action patterns

In animals at least, the responses which occur as displacement reactions are generally themselves fixed action patterns. This is important if they are to be used as information sources, since it means that they will be fairly reliable, being stereotyped in form and uniform across the species.

Consider now the case of a male and female of a distance species, both in mating condition. For reasons that we shall discuss in chapter 5, it is very important to females to mate only with males of their own species. Now suppose that the male, locked in his approach–avoid conflict, performs some displacement response. If that response is characteristic of males of his species, or if it displays some body structure (a patch of coloured feathers, perhaps) which is characteristic of males of his species, that will give the female good information that she can safely allow him to proceed to mate. This fact sets up a whole complex of pressures towards the evolution of a signalling instinct. There will be a selective advantage for females in waiting to see the crucial displacement reaction, and there will be a selective advantage for males in performing it sooner, more vigorously and more 'characteristically'. Given what we know from chapter 2 about sign stimuli, we might also suspect that if a characteristic body structure is involved, there will be a selective advantage for males who have it in larger, brighter or exaggerated form, or who display it more effectively by their displacement response. Furthermore, all these selective pressures will reinforce one another: the more females tend to wait for a displacement response to occur, the stronger the pressure on males to perform it, and the more surely males of their own species perform a given response, the stronger the pressure on females to reject any male who does not perform it. The situation has the potential for quite rapid evolution.

Lorenz (e.g. 1950) proposed that this kind of evolutionary process lies behind many of the fixed action patterns which seem to function as signals from one animal to another. Take 'courtship' as an example. Distance species commonly go through elaborate rituals before mating actually occurs. Tinbergen (1951) described the sequence for sticklebacks: when the female swims into a male's territory, he swims up to her in a series of loops called the 'zigzag dance'; she then swims round in front of him, whereupon he turns round and swims to the nest; she follows him down, which causes him to point his head at the nest entrance; she enters; this releases a quivering response from the male who thrusts his snout at the female's rump, causing her to spawn; the eggs then release fertilization from the male, and while this is happening the female swims away.

Similar sequences have been described for many species. Of course, they are not always adhered to rigidly (in my laboratory, male sticklebacks have been seen to grab passing females by the tail and yank them down to their nests). But the point is that the sequence can be analysed into a series of fixed action patterns, each of which produces a sign stimulus (often, like the stickle-back's red throat, a true releaser) for the next. Lorenz's proposal is that many of these fixed action patterns have their origins in displacement reactions. He suggested that the process of evolution involved would have two stages. In the first, the form of the displacement reaction would become standardized, both so as to display any relevant body features most effectively and because deviant performers would be selected against. Often the standard form produced would be exaggerated compared with the original, 'functional' form of the response. This process is usually called 'ritualization', a term which can be traced to Huxley (1914). At a second stage, the response, now in full use as a signal, would lose its connections with its original sign stimuli and motivation. Preening would no longer depend on the presence of foreign bodies in the feathers or fur: if it was an effective courtship signal, it would become attached to the sex drive rather than the 'care of the body surface' drive, and would be released by some sign stimulus from the female. In effect, a new IRM would have been formed. This motivational shift Lorenz called 'emancipation'.

The ideas of ritualization and emancipation are clever and plausible, but the case for their existence does not rest on that fact. The comparative method can be applied to demonstrate how courtship IRMs have evolved from displacement reactions. A well-known example, which we have already mentioned in passing, was studied by Desmond Morris (1959). As we saw earlier, zebra finches are apt to wipe their beaks when in the approach–avoid conflicts involved in mating. Zebra finches are members of a closely related group of tropical birds called grass finches. In two other grass finches, the striated finch and the spice finch, the same beak-wiping is seen, but in these two cases it has become ritualized and emancipated, and it is an effective courtship response. The beak-wipe occurs in exaggerated form as a response to the presence of the female and elicits sexual presentation from her.

Similar arguments about ritualization can be put through concerning displacement reactions that occur in aggression-versus-fear conflicts. We shall discuss this in more detail in the next chapter, but we can note now that there are selective advantages to an animal in abandoning a fight at an early stage if it has information that its opponent is the stronger of the two, or that the opponent is more likely to persist in fighting. Thus if a displacement reaction exposes a structure which is generally correlated with strength, or with willingness to escalate the fight, it is quite likely to cause the opponent to withdraw. This gives an obvious selective advantage and so creates the potential for ritualization and emancipation.

Responses other than displacement reactions can give rise to signalling instincts. The early ethologists made much of 'intention movements' (small movements which tend to occur just before, for example, flying off), but the processes of emancipation and ritualization are quite general. Any response that chances to give information about an animal's state or future behaviour is susceptable of being 'captured' by evolution and amplified into an instinct.

The inheritance of instincts

Lorenz's arguments about ritualization and emancipation are supported by comparative evidence. None the less, they all rest on an assumption which, so far, I have neither stated nor examined. I have assumed that instincts (in the sense of Lorenzian IRMs) can be passed from an animal to its descendants by genetic transmission.

We have already seen some evidence in favour of this assumption. In the first place, behaviour obviously does confer selective advantage and is often exquisitely adapted to the species' ecological niche. From a biological point of view, it would be odd if behaviour could not be acted upon by natural selection, and odder still if its adaptiveness was produced by any other means. Secondly, the comparative method provides evidence for the inheritance of behaviour: if the same responses occur in a group of closely related species, but do not in other, more distant species, the obvious explanation is that the members of those species have inherited the behaviour from a common ancestor. Thirdly, in a limiting sense, at least the potential for behaviour must be inherited. It is our different genes that give human beings highly opposable thumbs and spider monkeys highly prehensile tails, and this has much to do with the fact that spider monkeys rarely use pencils and humans rarely hang from ceilings with all four limbs waving in the air.

But all these lines of evidence are indirect. Can we show more directly that IRMs are inherited? In the majority of cases it is not obvious how we could go about it, but where opportunities for demonstrations exist they have been successful. Three examples are worth considering.

First is the case of the hygienic bees. Bee larvae sometimes die within capped cells of the honeycomb. In some strains of bees, the cells are uncapped and the dead larvae removed; other strains do not do this. At least where certain diseases are endemic, the 'hygienic' bees, who remove dead larvae, are at a substantial selective advantage, since unhygienic hives could be completely wiped out by infections spreading from dead larvae. By controlled mating between bees of different strains, Rothenbuhler (1964) was able to show that the uncapping and removal of dead larvae were both inherited according to straightforward Mendelian genetic principles of the sort that control human eye colour or blood group.

Second is the case of the incompetent hybrid parrots. Dilger (1962) carried out a comparative study of the innate releasing mechanisms of several species of parrots of the lovebird type. He then crossbred lovebirds of two different species, Fischer's lovebird from Tanzania, which carries nesting material in its beak, and the peach-faced lovebird from Namibia, which carries nesting material by tucking it into its feathers. Hybrids of the two species displayed a confused mixture of the two ways of carrying, which resulted in very little material reaching the nest site. Behaviour was here contributing to the infertility that is common in hybrids.

Perhaps it is not surprising that hybrids should show disrupted behaviour. The third example, which also concerns hybrids, is more impressive. Among the IRMs that Lorenz (1958) studied in ducks is the drake's 'head-up–tail-up' pattern, used in courtship: the drake dips his bill into the water, then lifts his head sharply, trailing water in the air. Many species of ducks show this pattern, but two, the Chiloe teal and the Bahama pintail, do not. Hybrids between these two species, however, do show the 'head-up–tail-up' response. The implication is that the genetic information required to specify the pattern was present in the parents, but not expressed: in the hybrid, for whatever reason, it emerges.

These examples are the stock in trade of ethology textbooks, and critics of a genetic approach to behaviour have rightly pointed to the way the same few examples are always quoted. However, there is no shortage of evidence that behaviour in general can be influenced by genetic factors. The reason these instances are so often cited is that they involve well-described Lorenzian IRMs, not just broad behavioural tendencies. They are demonstrations of the inheritance of instincts.

The selective advantage of signalling

Lorenz's idea of ritualization leads us to expect that animals will seem to 'make signals'. They will have fixed action patterns which tend to display brightly coloured, or distinctly shaped, parts of their bodies. The literature of ethology is full of examples of this. Many ducks have brightly coloured patches, called 'specula', on their wings (most readers will recall the mallard's purple speculum): to go with these, they have an exaggerated ritualized preening response which displays their specula to full effect. The stickleback and the European robin both have bright red throats: both have threat displays which involve presenting this throat full on to a rival. The herring gull has a bright red patch on its bill; with it, it has a fixed action pattern of standing behind its chick and presenting the bill right in front of the chick's eyes. Rabbits have white tails which contrast with their generally cryptic body colour; as they run along, they bob their tails up and down, which makes for maximum noticeability for any other rabbit following behind.

Young blue tits have brightly coloured throat linings: when their parents arrive at the nest, they open their beaks as widely as they can. The list could be continued indefinitely, and it certainly gives the impression that animals are, instinctively, making signals to each other.

As the work of the early ethologists became known among psychologists, it became common to think of such instinctive signalling as the simplest form of animal communication. This idea gained strength from the way the ethologists, especially Lorenz, tended to use the theory of natural selection. Lorenz (e.g. 1966, chapter 3) looked at the advantage that behaviour could confer on the species as a whole. Thus, if a threat response gives a rival the information that a cock robin on his own territory will fight persistently and violently, the species benefits if the rival withdraws without a fight: the resident is left to rear his young undisturbed, and the rival survives to look for unoccupied territory elsewhere.

The recent trend in the study of animal behaviour is to reject all such 'good of the species' arguments, on the grounds that the mathematics for them just does not work out: an animal with a gene for benefiting its species at a cost to itself would leave fewer descendants than one which puts its own advantage above that of the species. This is the argument of the sociobiologists, called by Dawkins (1976) the 'selfish gene' theory. From this perspective 'information transmission' does not seem quite the right way to look at signalling instincts. Instead, we should expect the instinctive signals animals make to tend to exploit other animals of the same species, to the advantage of the individual making the signal. Any advantage to the recipient of the signal should be quite incidental – though we should remember that the recipient, too, will be selected to read and exploit any signals that are around.

Where signals are sent from one species to another, we have no trouble in seeing them from this exploitative perspective. The angler fish dangles a lure just in front of its own mouth. Smaller fish see this, it releases food-catching responses in them, they dart at the lure – and are snapped up by the angler fish. We do not want to say that the angler fish is communicating with its prey, yet it is influencing their behaviour by exposing a body structure just as surely as a herring gull is influencing its chick's behaviour when it presents the chick with its red-spotted beak. Dawkins and Krebs

(1978) have suggested that we might think of instinctive signals as being like advertisements. Advertisers seek to influence people's behaviour – but in ways that suit their own interests, or their clients' interests, not necessarily the consumers'. They are not interested in sharing information, but in persuasion.

Of course, there are situations where the interests of both animals concerned in an exchange of signals seem to be the same. The herring-gull chick needs to feed if it is to survive and have descendants: the parent herring gull needs the chick to feed and survive if it is ever to have any grandchildren. Selective pressures acting on both parent gull and chick should therefore favour accurate communication of whether or not the parent has food available, and whether or not the chick needs it. However, as we shall see in chapter 5, a subtle disharmony of interests is quite possible even between parents and offspring. In other cases conflict of interest is blatant. In courtship, the male's interest lies in signalling to the female that he is extremely potent and competent, regardless of whether that is true. The female's interest lies in signalling to the male that any young she bears will be his, regardless of the truth of that proposition. In aggressive encounters, each party's interest lies in signalling that he (or she) is of overwhelming strength and determination, while being ready at any moment to abandon the fight and run if the evidence is that the other party is strong and resolute enough to do serious damage.

In a sociobiological analysis of signalling instincts, therefore, we should not ask ourselves how well they communicate from one animal to another. Rather, we should be considering how they will modify the behaviour of the animal that perceives them, and how, in the light of their effects, both the signal and the response to it can be maintained by natural selection.

Alarm calls and altruism

There is one kind of signalling instinct that poses particular problems for sociobiological analysis. This is the emission of signals when danger threatens. The most familiar examples are the alarm calls of small birds. I only have to step into my garden to elicit the sharp 'pink-pink' alarm call of the resident cock blackbird. Almost all songbirds have these calls, and as a matter of fact they are all rather similar (Marler, 1959), so that all species will respond when any one of them gives the alarm on seeing a human (or, more to the point perhaps, a cat or hawk).

This looks like a first-class example of 'good of the species' behaviour, in fact of a broader 'good of all birds in the garden' approach. The similarity of all birds' alarm calls is, however, easily explained – the characteristically drawn-out high note, with few overtones and a gradually falling pitch, turns out to be the hardest kind of sound for a two-eared predator to localize. But why should any animal give an alarm call at all, since giving even a hard-to-localize call must increase the risk that the caller will be the object of unwelcome attention from the predator? Nor is the phenomenon confined to garden birds: rabbits give the alarm by drumming with their feet on the ground, monkeys by screeching, and so forth.

The sociobiological account of alarm-calling draws upon the fact that the recipients of the signal are very possibly related to the signaller. Careful consideration shows that in any such case, the idea of signalling as relentless exploitation requires some modification. It has been said that the truly selfish animal should lay down its life for two brothers or eight cousins. The point is that an animal's selective advantage is served by any behaviour which ensures the survival of its genes into the next generation. The usual way of ensuring that your genes survive is to reproduce and rear your young. But your close relatives carry some of your genes too: on average, a full brother will have half of your genes. If, by dying, and so giving up entirely your own chances to reproduce, you make absolutely sure that more than two of your full brothers survive and reproduce, you have got what in evolutionary terms is a bargain (so long as you are discriminating enough about when you do it to make sure that your brothers do not show the same behaviour). Behaviours that lead to this sort of 'altruism' should therefore, according to the sociobiologists, tend to evolve.

The sociobiologists call this process 'kin selection', and the behaviours it produces 'kin altruism'. It is still a moot point whether alarm calls really are a case of kin altruism, but many other kinds of behaviour can be explained very convincingly in this way. The most extreme case is that of worker bees, who are sterile yet reproduce themselves indirectly by devoting all their efforts to rearing their sisters. We shall hear more of this in the next chapter.

Human signals: paralanguage

We have seen that animals' instinctive behaviours often modify the behaviour of other members of their species, and that this can be viewed as mutually advantageous communication, mutual exploitation, co-operation with a family, or some combination of all three. Are comparable processes at work in human beings, or has the development of language, a far more efficient means of communication (and of exploitation) led to the atrophy of simpler signalling instincts in our species?

In chapter 2, we mentioned a few reasonably well-documented cases of human IRMs, such as the head-turning response of newborn babies to a touch on the cheek and the eyebrow flash given on meeting an acquaintance. Interestingly, both of these are signalling instincts. In fact humans have a whole system of communication that exists in parallel with language. Technically it is usually referred to as 'paralanguage', though other terms (e.g. 'body language') are also used. Paralanguage embraces a wide range of phenomena, not all of them fitting the idea of a Lorenzian IRM at all well. My copy of the social psychologist Michael Argyle's book *Bodily Communication* (1975) has a picture on the cover of a girl giving a massive wink; and winking is obviously something we do as consciously and deliberately as talking. Other paralinguistic phenomena certainly fit the instinctual bill in being unintended: most of us would usually rather not blush, for instance, though blushing obviously serves to communicate something about our motivational state to whoever else is present. In fact there is a widespread impression that paralinguistic communication is harder to fake than language itself: we have phrases like 'his eyes did not confirm what his words said'. One of my colleagues once remarked of another, who is notoriously poker-faced, 'I couldn't tell what X really thought, he had shoes on so I couldn't see if his toes were twitching.'

The idea of paralanguage as a give-away of our real feelings does not fit very well with the idea of animals' instinctive communication as tending to deceive and exploit the recipient of the signal. Of course, we have to remember that what we perceive as our interests may not be what is favoured in evolution: girls who blush when spoken to by sexually aggressive males may leave more descendants than girls who do not; people whose voices shake when spoken to by bullies may be less likely to get into fatal fights than others who conceal their weakness better. Exploitation of an individual may be good for her or him, in evolutionary terms (though that certainly should not be taken as a moral justification for it). But in general, the idea that human paralanguage is the heir of animals' signalling instincts is not particularly well supported by data. There are some suggestive parallels, of course. Van Hooff (1962) related the human smile to the open-mouthed threat response shown by nearly all other primates (naturally this idea is favoured by those who see humour as being basically aggressive, at least in origin). Wolves have distinct postures and ways of walking according to their social status (Schenkel, 1947) and so do humans (e.g. Mehrabian, 1972). But at present these are mostly mere parallels. To go deeper than that we need a clearer understanding of the social function of communication, and to get that we need a clearer understanding of the biological nature of society itself. It is time to turn our attention from the evolution of instincts to the evolution of societies.

4

The evolution of societies

Most of the behaviours we have discussed so far are social, in the sense that they involve more than one animal. Look at the examples we have studied. A herring gull feeding its chick, a grass finch wiping its beak as a signal to a potential mate, even an oystercatcher brooding its egg – all these animals are involved in social behaviour.

Such social micro-instincts are the building blocks of the social life of animals. We could try to understand animal societies by starting with these simple behaviours between individuals and working up to wider relationships – what has been called a 'bottom-up' approach. While this has its place, there is an alternative way of looking at things that is also essential. Societies affect the lives of individuals. For example, a society that is organized into a hierarchy creates opportunities for individuals to struggle for and adopt dominant roles that would be meaningless in a more dispersed, less organized group.

This chapter takes the 'top-down' approach: it starts with societies as a whole, and asks how they affect the behaviours of individuals, and how they are produced by natural selection. In a few cases, we can approach the evolution of societies in the same way as the evolution of instincts, using the comparative method. The best-known example concerns the group of insects called the *Hymenoptera*, the ants, bees and wasps. As is well known, these include most of the 'social insects', nowadays more often called 'eusocial'. Eusocial species live in elaborate, differentiated societies within which each individual seems to work for the good of all. There are about 170,000 species of *Hymenoptera*, and sociality and eusociality exist in so many varieties among them that E.O. Wilson (1975, p. 415) has been able to estimate, by comparative methods, that eusociality has evolved at least eleven separate times within the group.

Such richness of comparative material is rare, and so it is equally rare for us to be able to draw such clear conclusions about the evolution of societies. Furthermore, there are good reasons why social structure will often depend more closely on animals' current ecological position than their evolutionary relationships, and this undermines the comparative method even when we have sufficient data to put it into effect. As a result, most of our discussion about the evolution of societies has to consist of working out what could have evolved rather than demonstrating what has evolved.

In consequence, the danger of armchair adaptationism is severe and everpresent in this chapter. There are two precautions we can take against it. First, we must be rigorous in trying to quantify the costs and benefits of different kinds of behaviour. Secondly, we must be specific about the genetic processes by which animals with an innate tendency to perform one kind of behaviour might come to replace animals with different or contrary innate tendencies.

Why do animals live in groups?

Animal species vary enormously in the extent to which members of the species consort with one another. Who has ever seen two herons fishing side by side? Yet, at the other extreme, we find herds of hundreds or thousands of antelope or buffalo, schools of hundreds of thousands of fish, and colonies of up to 22 million African driver ants. Furthermore, the amount of structure within groups also varies sharply. The flocks of seed-eating birds that form in autumn seem to be mere aggregations, in which each member of the group acts as an individual (Cody, 1971). At the other extreme, we have the eusocial insects, where from a single genetic blueprint individuals develop different body structures to fit them for particular roles within the society – worker, soldier or queen.

Why do some animals live in groups? Why is it precisely these species that do so? In answering these basic questions about the evolution of societies, we have to consider the advantage that the social life gives to each individual. It is the individual that is the carrier of the genetic material; it is on the survival of individuals that the perpetuation of any genetic innovation depends. From an individual point of view, there is one obvious factor that would seem to favour solitariness: to live with a group is to live with competitors for your food supply.

Sociobiologists have pointed to a number of factors that can none the less favour group-living. An obvious one is access to mates – sexually reproducing animals must have some contact with others of their kind. Other factors are more subtle, and most of them relate in some way to the relation between an animal, the food it eats, and the other animals for which it in turn is a potential meal.

Consider first the search for food. A group of animals acting together may have a number of advantages over an individual. First, members of a group may be able to report to each other where food is to be found: many readers will have heard of Von Frisch's (1966) famous discovery that honey bees perform a special 'waggle dance' to signal to one another the direction and distance of a nectar source. Secondly, a group acting together may be able to tackle larger prey than an individual could: among the cats, it is only lions that live in large social groups, and only lions that regularly prey on animals substantially larger than themselves, such as zebra, wildebeeste or waterbuck. But living in a group is not necessarily an advantage for the individual hunter. Although larger prey can be tackled, it also has to be shared, and we expect that individuals will compete for the largest share of their joint prize. In the lion pride, for example, it is the lionesses who are the efficient social hunters, but it is the males that take the lion's share of the prey (Schaller, 1972; Bertram, 1978). The group will be unstable unless the weakest lioness, who will get the smallest share, can get more food than she could by hunting alone. Group hunting, therefore, confers a possible but not an inevitable advantage, and the stable group size depends on a balance of interacting variables. Here we have precisely the sort of factor we need if we are to explain why some animals are social and others are not.

It is the same story when we consider animals as prey rather than predators. Groups have some obvious advantages when it comes to avoiding becoming someone else's dinner. A hundred pairs of eyes and ears are more likely to spot a predator coming than a single pair; by flying a trained goshawk at woodpigeons in flocks of various sizes, Kenward (1978) has shown that larger flocks take off sooner and are less likely to lose any member to the hawk than smaller groups. A large group may even be able to defend itself effectively: a flock of chaffinches will mob an owl or a hawk, which is not something a single chaffinch could attempt in any safety.

Once again, though, we have to consider the advantage to the individual within the group, not to the group as a whole. We saw in the previous chapter that alarm-calling poses severe problems when we take this individualistic standpoint, and much the same is true for group defence, though it is in any case a less widespread phenomenon. Washburn and DeVore (1961) reported that when a baboon troop was approached by a leopard, the large old males got between the danger and the vulnerable females and young, but in a later study (admittedly in different ecological conditions, and perhaps with different relationship patterns within the group) the large males were often the fastest to run away (Rowell, 1967). Are there really any processes that could predispose prey animals to live in groups even if they were acting for selfish individual advantage at every point?

Most predators attacking a group of prey animals take only one, or at any rate a very small proportion, of the group (man, obviously, is an exception). If only one member of a group is going to be taken, the larger the group, the lower the chance that any individual will be unlucky. Hamilton (1971) showed that an individual's chances of survival increase the closer it moves to the centre of a group. Here is a powerful, and purely individualistic, force that will tend to concentrate animals into groups.

On the other hand, living in a group may increase the danger from predators in other ways. A large group is much more likely to be spotted by a predator than a single individual, and once spotted it will present a more tempting target. From the point of view of avoiding predation, therefore, the optimal size of group for an individual to live in will again depend on a balance of variables. Once again we have the potential to explain why some animals live in groups and others do not.

Species, group, individual, kin and gene selection

In so far as genetic factors matter to behaviour, how a species behaves depends on the content of the 'gene pool' – the overall genetic make-up of the population. Evolution must therefore involve modifications to this gene pool. Such modifications can only come about by differential breeding success, that is by animals with one sort of gene having more descendants than animals with another sort of gene which competes with it, in the sense that one and only one of them can occupy a given position (locus) on an animal's chromosome. Note that what matters is *relative* breeding success. The total number of animals in the species is not at issue: what matters is the proportion of them whose genes are of a particular kind.

Two general propositions about social behaviour follow from this. The first is the basic biological prohibition against altruism: a gene which tells the animal bearing it to give up its own reproductive chances so that the total number in the species can increase will disappear in favour of more 'selfish' genes. The second, however, is the possibility of what we called in chapter 3 'kin altruism'. If a gene tells its owner to give up its own reproductive chances to ensure that three full brothers breed when otherwise they would have been barren, that gene will spread – since on average 1.5 of the brothers will be carrying it (each one having a half-chance to do so), and they will pass it on to their offspring. (Remember, however, that this works only if the gene comes into effect in relatively rare circumstances, since otherwise all the brothers would disappear in a riot of self-sacrifice.)

It is useful to know the terms biologists use to describe the different theoretical standpoints about evolution. The idea that behaviour (or any other property) will be perpetuated if it favours an entire group is called 'group selection'. The idea that only the good of the individual is relevant is called 'individual selection'. What we have seen in the last few paragraphs is that neither of these is really plausible. We know that evolution can produce behaviours that favour close relatives at the individual's expense: this process is called 'kin selection'. The underlying theory is that what is selected is not individuals, kin or groups, but genes. This idea is referred to as 'gene selection'.

There are a few rare circumstances where group selection may occur. The best-known empirical example concerns the myxoma virus, the micro-organism responsible for the disease myxomatosis, used to control rabbits. In both Britain and Australia, the myxoma virus has tended to get less virulent. This is surprising because reduced virulence means that the virus is reproducing less rapidly. Why should this be? Highly virulent strains of the virus kill the rabbits they infect extremely quickly. There is, therefore, little chance for a flea or mosquito to bite the rabbit before it dies. Less virulent strains kill the rabbit more slowly, and so give the fleas and mosquitoes a chance to bite it and then bite other rabbits and pass on the infection (Fenner, 1965). Now, an infected rabbit is, in effect, a colony of viruses. Within that colony, any virus that reproduces exceptionally fast will be at an advantage over its fellow members, and so should be favoured by individual selection. But as soon as this selective pressure takes too strong an effect, the entire colony is doomed, since its members will kill their host before it can carry them within range of a new host. The colony can only survive if none of its members reproduces too fast. This is group selection, and it can work in this case because groups are liable to die out faster than individuals: it can be shown mathematically that this is the key condition. Notice that even in the myxoma virus, selection does not act to procure the good of the entire species, it just moves to act on a slightly less parochial scale than that of the individual virus.

Not only is there no way that selection can produce behaviours that favour the species at the individual's expense, but often it will produce behaviours that are disadvantageous to the species. For example, many animals compete either for food or for mates, and in nearly all such competitions, the larger of two animals will be at an advantage. There is thus a general selective pressure towards increasing size. From the species' point of view, however, this is

53

nearly always a bad thing. Theoretically, large size looks like a disadvantage: if one elephant is killed by a disease, the species has lost several tons of its total mass; if one mouse suffers the same fate only a few grams are lost. Empirical evidence amply supports this. To look at the fossil relatives of almost any group of animals is to find giants – penguins 5 feet tall, and so forth. Clearly these large species were not successful. Similarly, where whole groups of species have developed large size, they become endangered. Both the horse and the elephant families are much less significant among the whole spectrum of mammals than they once were. Thus selective pressures on individuals tend to produce large size, which in turn tends to drive the species towards extinction.

But if this is so, it may be argued, why do not all species of animals become extinct? The short answer is that they do. The great majority of species that have ever existed are already extinct, and extinction awaits the surviving species as surely as death awaits individuals. Obviously this is only part of the story, since some species do give rise to their successors. There is a sense in which there is a competition between species just as there is a competition between genes. What species can we expect to win this competition? The answer would seem to be those where what favours the survival of an individual relative to his or her fellows also favours the survival of his or her species relative to other species. Species where it is to an individual's advantage to be small, for example, might expect a relatively long run before extinction catches up with them. Although the comparative ethologists touched on it (e.g. Tinbergen, 1951, p. 204), sociobiologists have hardly begun to study this kind of 'species selection' (Stanley, 1975); Dawkins (1982, pp. 101–9) provides the only relevant discussion. Yet we clearly need to get to grips with species selection if we are to understand why we have the species that we do have, as well as why each species has the individuals that it has.

Aggressive and appeasement responses

The theory of natural selection leads us to expect competition between individuals, and if we look at animal behaviour, we see plenty of what looks like aggression between members of the same species. The problem of finding a precise definition for 'aggression' has filled many columns of the learned journals, but by and large we can rely on the evidence of our senses: what looks like a squabble between two animals usually is. Of course, it is possible to be misled if you do not know the species in question very well. Before the present century, few people realized that most bird song is a kind of threat behaviour. But it is an obvious fact that most animals are sometimes aggressive towards others of their species.

However, two highly misleading myths about animal aggression are in circulation. One may be called the 'nature red in tooth and claw' myth, the idea that animals will show unrestrained aggression towards each other under virtually any circumstances, on a scale and with a ferocity unknown in human life. Most people realize that this is no more than a myth as soon as they think about it. The second myth is more dangerous because it springs from scientific writings. It has been widely claimed, especially by Lorenz (1966) and Eibl-Eibesfeldt (1979), that animal aggression is unlike human aggression, in that animals never actually kill members of their own species: a fight always stops before serious damage is done. On this basis humans are seen as uniquely and viciously aggressive. As we shall see, this idea too is false. But there is some truth behind it, which is why it is appropriate to think of it as a myth rather than simply as a mistake.

Many of the innate releasing mechanisms that Lorenz and Tinbergen studied are involved with aggression. Few of them concern actual fighting, however. The great majority of aggressive IRMs are signalling micro-instincts of the sort whose evolution we considered in chapter 3. Generally these are referred to as threat responses. For example, when a male stickleback sees another male, he will posture with his head downwards, at the bottom of the water, showing his red throat; and a herring gull whose nesting site is invaded by another gull will adopt an upright posture, with wings slightly open at the shoulder and beak pointing down and towards the trespasser – what Tinbergen (1959) called the 'upright threat' response.

Once such a threat has been made, one of three things may occur. The threatened animal may make a threat response in return. Alternatively, it may simply run, swim or fly away. Most commonly, however, it will respond with a different fixed action pattern, which has the effect of terminating the conflict but allowing the threatening animal to proceed as though it has 'won'. In effect, the threatened animal has 'surrendered'. The responses used to signal surrender are called 'appeasement responses'.

Examples of appeasement responses abound in the literature of ethology. A rat submitting to a threat from a stronger rat will crawl under the aggressor's stomach (Barnett, 1958). A herring gull submitting to an 'upright threat' from another gull will adopt an almost opposite posture, with shoulders hunched, beak horizontal, facing away from the aggressor (it is easy to see both upright threat and the corresponding appeasement response around any British coast, especially in autumn, when the juvenile gulls, still in brown plumage, are constantly having to appease adults). In many primates, males and females alike appease a threat by making a version of the female's sexual-presentation response; often the threatening animal (male or female) will acknowledge this appeasement response by mounting the appeaser.

This last appeasement response has another point of interest. As anyone who has visited a zoo will know, female baboons have brightly coloured backsides, which are offered towards the male both in sexual presentation and when pseudo-presentation is used as an appeasement response. The interesting point is that in the hamadryas baboon this 'sexual skin' develops long before the female is sexually mature and able to mate; furthermore, juvenile males have it as well. Its only function in juveniles is, apparently, in appeasement: it is a releaser in the strict sense. This shows that the selective pressures tending to produce appeasement responses are strong enough to drive the evolution of body structures with no other use. It is not the only example: male spotted hyenas have an appeasement display involving the penis, and in female hyenas the clitoris is expanded into a convincing-looking pseudo-penis which is used in the same display and apparently at no other time (Kruuk, 1972).

But what selective pressures could produce appeasement responses? It is easy to see how Lorenz could have been led to think in terms of the good of the species. Superficially, there seems no reason why an aggressor should not proceed to finish off a rival once it had conceded defeat. From an individual selectionist point of view, surely the best strategy for a successful aggressor is to proceed to finish off a rival who has conceded defeat, since that would remove all chance of future competition. If aggressors regularly did that, appeasement responding would disappear, for the selective advantage would lie with animals which went on fighting to the death, even if they only had a tiny chance of winning.

The key to an understanding of this problem has been provided by Maynard Smith (e.g. 1976) who used the mathematical theory of games to develop the concept of an evolutionarily stable strategy (ESS). We need not bother with the mathematics here, as the major idea is quite simple. Provided that an animal that has shown an appeasement response will return to the fight if and only if it is further attacked, then the best strategy for the aggressor is to call off the fight once the rival has surrendered. For if the winner carries on the fight, there is a risk (however small) that he will in the end be defeated. There is a much greater risk that he will be injured sufficiently badly to impair either his life expectancy or his reproductive chances, and there is a virtual certainty that while he is engaged in the fight, he will be losing time and energy that he could be using in gathering food or protecting his mates. The upshot is that no mutation can confer a selective advantage once the gene pool contains a high proportion of genes for appeasing if attacked by a stronger rival, accepting appeasement if offered and fighting on if appeasement is rejected.

Some of these processes have been observed at work by Clutton-Brock, Albon, Gibson and Guinness (1979) in a study of red deer on the Scottish island of Rhum. During the rut (breeding season), mature red deer stags gather together small groups of hinds ('harems'), which they defend in roaring contests with other males. Normally, in such contests, whichever stag is less able to roar loudly and continuously will eventually withdraw, possibly leaving the other in command of his harem. Occasionally, especially when roaring capacity seems to be well matched, an escalated fight will ensue. Clutton-Brock and his colleagues showed that the costs of such fights could be severe, even to the winner. In a few cases, stags lost eyes or broke legs, and these animals did not survive many months. Antlers were often broken, and a stag without antlers has reduced breeding success. The greatest costs, however, came in lost hinds. While two harem-holding stags were fighting, with their antlers locked together, the hinds could be chased away and mated by less mature, non-harem-holding males. Thus, for a stag that had won a roaring contest, to pursue the defeated rival would obviously impose considerable costs (in terms of lost descendants) for no advantage.

It follows from Maynard Smith's theory that if aggression can be carried through without serious risk, appeasement would not be accepted if offered, and so is unlikely to evolve. An example of this occurs in lions (Schaller, 1972; Bertram, 1978). Lions' permanent social groups are 'prides' of related lionesses, accompanied by one to three male lions, who are related to each other but not to the females. Young females born into a pride are normally recruited into it when they become sexually mature, but young males leave. They wander away from the pride, usually as a group of two or three brothers or cousins, until they reach their peak size and strength at an age of about 3 years. They then find a pride (not usually the one they were born into) and drive out the males associated with it; they will remain with that pride, and father cubs in it, until they are themselves driven out. When a new group of males succeeds in taking over a pride, the defending lions submit and withdraw, and are not further attacked. But the incoming males will often attack and kill any cubs present in the pride. The selective pressure producing this behaviour is fairly obvious: the incoming males will only have a few years with the pride before they will themselves be dislodged. If existing cubs are killed, the lionesses will stop lactating, and so will be ready to mate with the newcomers several months sooner. Furthermore, the cubs cannot offer any effective resistance, and so there is no pressure on the incoming males to respond to any appeasement behaviours the cubs might show.

Infanticide is one of the commoner kinds of unrestrained aggression among animals, and in many cases it occurs where permanent female groups are taken over by successive unrelated males. Sarah Blaffer Hrdy (1977, chapter 8) has studied it in an Indian monkey species, the Hanuman langur, and she lists many reports of similar behaviour in other primates. Is it fanciful to see a link from this to the 'wicked stepmother/father' theme so common in European folk stories? Perhaps it is; but it is true that child abuse is commoner in families where a stepparent is present (Daly and Wilson, 1981). It is not unreasonable to suppose that there is some instinctual component in attacks on the child of a sexual partner's previous relationship.

Infanticide among langurs is a good example of behaviour that serves the individual's selective advantage while being bad for the species. In one langur troop Hrdy studied, only two out of twelve infants born over a thirty-eight-month period survived. Three of the others were seen being killed by incoming males, and the rest probably suffered the same fate, since they disappeared at times of male take-over. This high rate of loss occurs even though the females show several behaviour patterns which appear to be explicitly adapted to resist male aggression against infants.

Thus while animal aggression does involve much more posturing and formal contest than actual fighting, this is not because animals are seeking the greatest good of their species. Where unrestrained aggression can serve individual selective advantage, it will occur.

Human aggression

How does human aggression fit into this pattern? It could be that humans are simply a rather aggressive kind of animal. Some species do seem much more aggressive than others, mainly because they are not well equipped with appeasement responses. Peaceful animals like wolves can be kept closely confined together in small cages; highly aggressive ones, like doves, have to be kept one to a cage or they will peck one another to death. There are two reasons why a species might not have many appeasement responses. As in male langur behaviour towards infants, the pattern of interrelationships in the animal's natural social groups may not encourage appeasement responses to evolve. Alternatively, flight rather than appeasement may be the usual way of abandoning a fight – doves can be kept together perfectly well in an aviary where there is room for a defeated bird to fly out of the victor's way, for a dove that flies away will not be harassed further.

Could it be the case that humans are not well equipped with appeasement responses, and that modern life so crowds us together that we are unable to get out of the way of aggressors? This really does not seem plausible. First, what are cringing, crying and begging if they are not appeasement responses? Secondly, as the social psychologist Jonathan Freedman (1975) points out, there is no consistent evidence that crowding makes people in general more aggressive. Would you rather meet a potential New York mugger at night on the dirty, crowded sidewalks of Broadway, or in the much more salubrious but deserted streets one block to the east or west? The answer is obvious. Of course, it could be that people *feel* more aggressive in crowds, but are more likely to restrain aggressive behaviour, but Freedman shows that the evidence in favour of this is weak.

Lorenz and Eibl-Eibesfeldt suggest an alternative explanation of human aggression. They argue that human appeasement responses are normally very effective. We know that there are people around who can kill other people in cold blood and with their bare hands. But these are exceptions, as rare as they are repellent. What makes humans appear so much more aggressive than other animals, Lorenz argues, is our technology. Even a crude weapon like the leg-bone of an antelope is capable of killing a rival without giving him a chance to emit an appeasement response. It is unthinkable that the airmen who released atomic bombs on Hiroshima and Nagasaki, or the politicians who stand ready to order the release of a holocaust thousands of times more destructive, could personally and without weapons kill millions of men, women and children who were present in front of them begging and pleading to be spared. Human instinct would not allow it.

The early ethologists embedded this argument within a 'good of the species' framework. We have to reject that framework, but that is no reason to reject the argument. Humans may well be more aggressive than some other animals; Hrdy's discussion of infanticide suggests that may be a common trait of social primates. But the quite exceptional damage we do to our own species is most plausibly explained by the fact that we have developed a technology which enables our intentions to override our instincts. It is a sobering thought that, as Ardrey (1961) has suggested, this may have been the driving force behind the development of technology from the earliest times, as it certainly has been this century.

Affiliative responding

Aggressive and appeasement responses are together known as 'agonistic' behaviours. For a variety of reasons, they have preoccupied both the early comparative ethologists and the more recent sociobiologically inclined theorists. But animal societies do not consist only of networks of threat and submission. There are also responses that are used as signs of what we may call 'affection'; to be less anthropomorphic, we can say that their function is to maintain a relationship between two individuals.

The most obvious of these is simple touching, or being in touch. I referred in chapter 3 to Hediger's distinction between 'distance' and 'contact' species. With some contact species, any number of animals sharing living space will be found in contact with each other. Rats are like this: in my laboratory I keep rats in groups of twenty or so in large cages, and if you go into the keeping room while they are asleep, you will always find all twenty in one arbitrarily chosen corner, in one great ball of fur, tails, noses and whiskers. Other contact species are more discriminating. Some species of monkeys, for example, have 'sitting together' relationships: two animals will spend their resting hours sitting together on a perch or branch, limbs or tails entwined, not doing anything in particular.

Another very common affiliative response is grooming. Mammals and birds spend a considerable amount of time preening, scratching and washing their fur or feathers. Sometimes they do it for themselves, and this obviously has the function of cleansing the body surface though, as we saw in chapter 3, it is also a common displacement response and readily becomes ritualized into a signal. Often, however, animals groom one another. This too may be useful in removing dirt or parasites (the comparative psychologist Wolfgang Köhler, 1927, p. 310, reported that chimpanzees will remove splinters from one another's hands by squeezing with their nails, and one of his chimpanzees even removed a splinter for him). But, at least among primates, grooming has a far more important function in maintaining social relations. Primate species tend to have definite patterns of grooming relations. Rhesus monkeys have small 'cliques' whose members all prefer grooming one another to grooming non-members (Sade, 1972). In other species, animals of higher status always groom lower status animals, or (more commonly) vice versa. There may also be sex limitations, so that females groom males but not vice versa.

Very similar patterns have been observed in humans. Using Inquisition records, Le Roy Ladurie (1980) has constructed a fascinating picture of fourteenth-century life in the Pyrenean village of Montaillou. A common social activity was for people to sit inside or outside their houses, delousing each other. In Montaillou, delousing was always from lower to higher status.

Men (dominant at the time) were always deloused by women, mothers by daughters, and so forth. But delousing was not an expression of dominance: Le Roy Ladurie calls it 'an ingredient of friendship' (p. 141). While delousing is nowadays more a medical than a social behaviour, we see something similar in the way girls of nine or ten in our culture spend time fingering or combing their friends' hair.

More complex affiliative responses, clearly fitting the Lorenzian concept of IRMs, have been studied in birds. A mutual display, usually called the 'ecstatic', is shown in one form or another by every species of penguin that has been studied. In the jackass penguin, for example, both members of a pair bray with their beaks turned upwards and their heads and upper parts thrust towards each other. These displays may serve an agonistic function, advertising the pair or family's ownership of a nest site, but their major function seems to be to cement the relationships between the birds joining in them.

Simple social structures

If one animal shows a threat response towards another, and the threatened animal replies with an appeasement response, we say that the first animal is 'dominant' and the second 'submissive'. In some species, dominance relationships between animals either remain constant or are highly predictable as a function of time or place. In such cases, it is possible to analyse the social structure in terms of networks of dominance relationships. There are two kinds of social structure which can be described quite well in this 'bottom-up' fashion.

The first of these has been mentioned several times in this book. There are many species where individuals or family groups hold and defend an area of space within which they find food and rear their young. Such defended areas are called 'territories'. While territoriality is by no means as widespread as one might suppose from reading popular ethology books, it is fairly common, especially in birds and coastal or river fish. Furthermore, territory-holders are often brightly coloured, or noisy, so they include some of the species best known to the layman. We have already encountered the stickleback (brightly coloured), the gibbon (very noisy indeed) and the robin (brightly coloured and noisy); other examples include blackbirds, the Siamese fighting fish, the great tit, the vividly coloured Anolis lizard and many species of hummingbirds.

In chapters 2 and 3, I referred to territory-holders as being fearful when off their territories and aggressive when on them. A simpler way of describing territoriality is to say that a territory-holder is dominant on his or her territory and submissive off it. Many of our examples of signalling instincts come from the threats and appeasements shown by territorial animals, since in good habitat territories will be packed closely together and boundary disputes will be common; and the fortunes of the participants will fluctuate as the contest strays across territorial boundaries.

The other easily described social structure is what is technically described as a 'dominance hierarchy' but is known to the wider world as a 'pecking order'. The phrase was coined by the Norwegian comparative psychologist Schjelderup-Ebbe (1922), who was studying dominance relations in a flock of hens. He found that, at least in small flocks, there was an exact, linear dominance order. This means that there is one hen (usually referred to as the alpha hen) who can peck any other hen without retaliation, and periodically exercises this 'peck right'; beneath her is a 'beta' hen, who can and occasionally does peck at any hen except the alpha; and so on down to an 'omega' hen who is liable to be pecked by any other hen and can never retaliate.

Schjelderup-Ebbe's work attracted much attention. Dominance hierarchies certainly are a property of groups of chickens; indeed, they are a factor of some importance in the husbandry of many farm animals. They are also relatively easily observed in zoos. Unfortunately, like territory, dominance hierarchy is too easily assumed to be ubiquitous. The danger of this assumption is the graver because it is just the conditions that make animals easiest to observe (i.e. captivity or providing a single, focused food source) that seem likely to induce a hierarchy in animals that do not normally show one (e.g. baboons: Rowell, 1967). But dominance hierarchies do sometimes occur in natural conditions. Deag (1977) found that wild barbary apes show a clear hierarchy. Collias, Collias, Hunsaker and Minning (1966) studied the red jungle fowl that run more or less wild in the San Diego zoo in California. Flocks of birds held territories, but within flocks there were quite strict dominance hierarchies. This example is crucial, because the Burmese red jungle fowl is the ancestor of the domestic chicken.

More complex social structures

The majority of animal societies do not live in dominance hierarchies or on fixed territories. Their social structures are therefore hard to define in terms of dominance relationships between pairs of individuals. How can they be described?

In many cases, the key factor is the way in which males and females are linked in temporary or permanent sexual relationships, and we shall be looking at the possibilities this raises at the end of this chapter and in chapter 5. However, there are a few additional concepts which it will be helpful to introduce here.

Even if they do not have territories, animals usually live in defined places. The area that an animal or a group habitually uses is called its 'home range'. In classically territorial animals, the home range and the territory are more or less identical, but in more complex social structures this is not the case. Herring gulls, for example, defend a small territory around their nesting sites, but their home range also includes the various feeding places that they visit in common with numerous other gulls. At the feeding sites, agonistic encounters may occur over particular pieces of food, but not over the use of space as such. Many group-living primates have home ranges that overlap with those of neighbouring groups; typically, the two groups will not use the overlap area simultaneously, a mutual avoidance that may be mediated by special calls (as in howler monkeys) which do not seem to be agonistic. Where home ranges overlap, animals often have what is called a 'core area' within which a disproportionate amount of activity is concentrated. Different groups' core areas do not usually overlap, but again this seems to be because of mutual avoidance rather than territorial defence.

Relations within groups are also usually more complex than simple ideas about territory and dominance would suggest. Even strictly territorial animals usually have at least a minimal social grouping, of mother and her young, and there may be structure above that level. For example, among water voles, Leuze (1980) found 'nested' male and female territories, with the male defending a large territory against other males but not females, and within his territory two or three females defending territories against other females but not against the male. Orang-utans have the same sort of structure except that they have undefended home ranges instead of defended territories. Another twist is provided by the American jaçana, a marshland bird in which females maintain large territories against other females. Within these, several males maintain territories against one another, make nests and rear young from eggs laid in their nests by the female (Jenni, 1974).

In larger groups the most important relationships are usually sexual, but two other important social building blocks are worth mentioning. One is sibling groups. All the females in a lion pride or langur troop are closely related – they are at least equivalent to first cousins (Bertram, 1976; Hrdy, 1977, appendix 3). In brush turkeys, females are courted by pairs of males, only one of which will ultimately mate with the hen: these pairs are brothers (Watts and Stokes, 1971).

The other common building block is what is called a 'matriline', which is a group consisting of a female, her sexually mature daughters (and possibly granddaughters) and the dependent young of all of them. In one way or another, matrilines form part of almost all primate societies (gibbons are an exception, being territorial, and so is the hamadryas baboon, in which the female leaves her natal group to join a male).

The selective pressures which tend to form both these sub-groupings should be obvious. Living in groups can confer advantages on individuals, as we saw in the early sections of this chapter. But to move into, or stay in, a group does not simply win an advantage for yourself; it also gives an advantage to the other members of the group. If those other members are your close relatives, you can as it were claim back some of the advantage you give them: some of their genes are your genes, and so their genetic advantage is (to a diminished extent, to be sure) your genetic advantage.

Food, females and the evolution of societies

We have looked at a considerable range of selective pressures that have an effect on social behaviour. Is it possible to achieve any integrative view of them, beyond the simple generalizations about gene selection which we have already considered in this chapter?

Wrangham (1979) argues that, regardless of variations between species, certain principles can be relied upon. The first is that, for the females, the limiting resource will be food. What a female is, at the most basic level, is a device for turning food into offspring (readers who find this description unflattering should wait till I come to males). The distribution of females will therefore depend on the distribution of food, and this will depend on what counts as food for that species.

The second general principle is that, for the males, the limiting resource is not food but females. What a male is, at the most basic level, is a parasite upon one or more females: he uses their food-gathering capacity to generate offspring for which he does not provide the food (see?). The distribution of males will therefore depend upon the distribution of females, just as that in turn depends on the distribution of food.

Finally, the actions of the males will alter the distribution of the females; the actions of both males and females may alter the distribution of food; and these effects will react back upon the distribution of both males and females.

We have here a set of general principles which we can apply to try to understand the selective pressures that maintain almost any animal society. A good example is the behaviour of sunbirds. Sunbirds are the African equivalents of humming birds, that is they feed on nectar (though they do not hover). Some species, but not all, are territorial. Others are territorial some of the time. A fine analysis of one of the latter, the Malachite sunbird, has been carried out by Wolf (1975). Sunbirds feed almost entirely on nectar, and it is possible to work out quite exactly how much the flowers on a particular bird's territory are worth to it, in terms of the energy that can be obtained from the nectar in them. It is also possible to measure how much energy a sunbird uses in flying around its territory to keep intruders off. Wolf observed that the birds he was watching defended their territories strictly during the morning and evening, but tolerated intruders during the afternoon. The nectar supply in the flowers from which the birds were feeding is high in the mornings. By the afternoon it is low, as the birds have taken most of it, but it builds up again by evening. Calculations showed that in the afternoon, the birds would have used more energy in defending their territories than they could have gained by retaining exclusive access to the flowers on it. In the morning or evening, however, territorial defence was definitely worthwhile.

This is an excellent example of the way in which access to food determines social structure. But note that it is *male* Malachite sunbirds that maintain territories, and therefore, apparently contradicting Wrangham's principles, it is the male here who is being affected by food distribution – what happens is that females are attracted to territory-holding males, so that for the males to procure the resource they need (females), they have to provide the resource the females need (food). So even this simple case is made complex by the relations between the sexes. These are now overdue for examination, and we shall consider them in the next chapter.

5

Males, females and offspring

We have already made passing references to the differences in behaviour between male and female animals. This chapter looks at them in detail. Many sex differences (though not all) centre on the production and care of offspring, and so this chapter is also concerned with the ways in which animals, male and female, care for their young, and the instincts and social structure that support that care. As we saw in chapter 4, the relationships between the sexes, and between adults and juveniles, are crucial elements in social structure, and so this chapter also continues our discussion of the different kinds of society found in the animal kingdom.

What is a male? What is a female?

It is surprisingly hard to find any property that can be used, throughout the animal kingdom, to distinguish males from females. For the purposes of analysing behaviour, however, there is one characteristic that seems to be fundamental. It goes to the core of sexual reproduction, which involves each of two individuals contributing a special reproductive call called a 'gamete' to the new organism. We shall define a female as an animal that contributes a gamete which contains both genetic information and a store of food (i.e. an energy source) for the new organism. Such a gamete is called an 'ovum', or 'egg'. A male, on the other hand, will be defined as an animal that contributes a gamete containing only genetic information. Such a gamete is called a 'sperm'. The store of food the egg contains may be large (as in most birds) or small (as in most fish or in mammals), but in either case it is easy to show that once egg-producing organisms exist, there will be a selective pressure towards the production of sperm-producers which can, as it were, steal a free ride for their genes on the energy source provided by the female. In this fundamental sense, males are always parasites: sperm treat eggs almost in the way viruses treat the cells of their hosts.

This way of defining the two sexes is consistent with the way we usually assign gender in all the familiar groups of animals. Thus, in this book at least, we need not think of it as a definition but as a property of male and female. The name for this property is 'anisogamy', which simply means having different-sized gametes.

An astonishing range of consequences follows from the fundamental fact of anisogamy. It puts males and females under subtly different selective pressures, which can be used to explain almost all the commonly noticed differences between the behaviour of the two sexes. Why is this? The point is that, at the moment when egg and sperm meet and a new organism is created, the female parent has committed more resources than the male to the building of her gamete. If anything now goes wrong with that offspring, the cost to the female of getting back to the same position will be higher. This means that the balance of costs and benefits for any behaviour is different for the two sexes: the female will be under stronger selective pressure to provide care for the offspring. According to the sociobiologists, this is why, for example, female mammals have evolved to retain their offspring inside their bodies for weeks or months. Such physiological adaptations greatly reinforce the fundamental bias created by anisogamy when it comes to the determination of behaviour: by the time a human infant is born, its mother has contributed very substantial amounts of time and food to its growth, while from a physiological standpoint its father need only have contributed a few sperm, practically costless in energy terms. It will cost the mother much more than the father to get back to the same point if the baby dies, and the mother is, therefore, under much stronger selective pressure to continue caring for the baby than the father is.

As we shall see later in the chapter, anisogamy does not completely determine the roles that will be taken up by the two sexes. There are reversals of the usual pattern. Nor should it be taken as providing moral justification for the assignment of particular roles to human males and females – the question of what kind of social structure is natural for humans is an open one, as we shall see at the end of this chapter and in chapter 7, and in any case to say that something is 'natural' is never a justification. What anisogamy does do is to create a consistent evolutionary bias, tending to push males and females towards different physiological and behavioural adaptations. We shall consider some of the outworkings of this bias in the rest of this chapter.

Male display, female choice: why do peacocks have tails and grouse have leks?

Before offspring can be formed, male and female must find each other and form a relationship, at least for long enough to copulate, and for much longer in many species. For widely dispersed, solitary animals, it may be quite a problem for males and females to find each other, and ethologists have discovered many instincts that are useful in this respect. Usually they involve auditory signals (an example is the cuckoo's call) or chemical communication: animals, especially insects and mammals, have been shown to be equipped with a surprising range of special secretory cells which deposit specific substances (generally referred to as 'phero-mones') in the environment. In the Noctuid moths, for example, as Von Frisch (1926) showed, the female releases into the air a chemical which is sufficient both to attract the male and to elicit copulation – even with the object from which a female has just taken off. Many mammals have scent glands which incorporate pheromones into their urine or faeces; others have glands that enable them to rub pheromones on to any surface – this is what your cat is doing, for example, when it rubs its face or its flanks 'affectionately' against your legs.

But in most species, when the time comes for breeding, there will be a considerable number of males and females present in the same neighbourhood, and the question to be asked is how particular males come to mate with particular females. There are species where the answer seems to be brute force – red deer stags, bull elephant seals and male hamadryas baboons, for example, all seem to herd together whatever females they can find, the females having no opportunity to escape (we shall see shortly that perhaps they would not take such an opportunity, however). More commonly it seems that the female has some degree of choice. Why should she take one male rather than another?

Part of the answer can be derived directly from anisogamy. When a female accepts a mate, she is giving to the partnership something that is, for her, expensive – the energy-rich egg. It is therefore a serious matter for her if the egg is wasted. And it will be wasted if the mating is with a male of another species, since the outcome is likely to be an infertile hybrid. There is, then, quite a strong selective pressure on the female to wait to mate until she has seen something from the male which guarantees that he is of the right species. We saw in chapter 3 how this need for caution on the female's part could drive the ritualization of displacement reactions into signalling instincts. Clearly, females will choose only those males who show the correct 'courtship' responses.

This is only the beginning of the story, however. If two males both make courtship responses towards the same female, which will she choose? From what we know about innate releasing mechanisms, we expect that it will be the one with the brightest releasing stimuli, the most exaggerated display and the greatest persistence. We should not be surprised, therefore, by the existence of species such as the peacock, where the males indulge in purely formal contests, displaying their remarkable tails to any peahens who are around. Indeed, it is easy to see how structures like the peacock's tail can evolve: those males with larger and more splendid tails will presumably attract the peahens more strongly, and so will leave more descendants. Furthermore, once this begins to be true, there will be a selective pressure on peahens to choose mates with splendid tails, since (provided that tail splendour is heritable), the sons of such peacocks should also have splendid tails, and so should ensure that the peahen has many grandchildren. A positive feedback loop is thus completed, and it is not hard to see how an insignificant releaser used in courtship could rapidly evolve into something really remarkable, such as the peacock's tail.

Not all animals have contests that involve the display of body structure. Another instructive system of female choice occurs in several species of grouse, and is called a 'lek'. A scattering of other birds, a number of species of fish (Loiselle and Barlow, 1978) and at least one antelope (the Uganda kob: Buechner and Roth, 1974) show the same sort of behaviour. The males of lekking species do not fight for females as such. Mating takes place at the same place (the lekking ground) season after season, and within this area the males fight for control of small areas of territory, which seem to have no value in terms of resources. These are the leks themselves. The females then select as mates whichever males are holding the central leks, which are the ones that are most hotly contested.

Once again it is easy to see how selective pressures will act to maintain this system (not quite as easy to see how it could originate). The pressure on the males to fight for the central lek is obvious; the pressure on the females to choose the holder of the central lek comes from the fact that his sons are likely to be successful fighters, and so good sources of grandchildren for them. The lek, in fact, is a sort of externalized peacock's tail.

The majority of animal species do not have elaborate structures like peacock's tails, nor do they fight for leks. But these extremes help to explain what is going on in apparently more mundane cases. Much more common than the lek is the situation where animals hold territories with resource value, and often these play a part in mate selection. Among kittiwakes, for example, which like most gulls hold nesting territories, the males arrive in the nesting area somewhat earlier in the season than the females. They establish themselves, with considerable squabbling, on nesting sites. When the females arrive, the males stand on their nests and emit a special cry (the 'long call'), which serves to attract potential mates. What is happening here? Are the females choosing the best nest site, and accepting whatever male happens to have it? Or are they choosing the best nest site because the male who has it must be a successful fighter and will have sons who will in their turn be able to hold territories that will be attractive to females? The case of the lek warns us that this second selective pressure may be as relevant as the first.

The lek analogy may help to explain an apparent paradox about territorial behaviour. In general we expect resources to be critical to territory size – the richer the habitat, the smaller the territories animals will hold. Yeaton and Cody (1974) counted the number of species of small seed-eating birds present on each of thirty islands off the British Columbian coast, and showed that where the song sparrow was the only such species it had quite small territories, while territories were many times larger when there were many (up to thirteen) competing species. This looks like a neat demonstration of the effects of ecological circumstances on territory, but pause a moment and consider it. The most important competitor for food, to a song sparrow, is not any other species of seed-eater, but another song sparrow. Why do the birds react to competitors of their own species by driving them out of their territory, but to competitors of other species by increasing their territory size? The most obvious answer is that although the song sparrow's territory does provide resources of food, shelter and nesting sites, it also has something of the function of a lek. Other song sparrows are potential competitors for mates, while other species are competitors only for food and shelter.

Similar considerations explain another odd fact about territoriality. Blackbirds maintain quite rigid territories: if I look out of my office window at the large lawn in front of the building I work in, I do not have to wait many minutes to see a territorial dispute at any time during the blackbird breeding season. Yet, so long as they are merely feeding, blackbirds can sometimes wander across territorial boundaries without the resident raising any protest. David Lack (1954) comments on the same phenomenon in robins.

The early ethologists were inclined to see territoriality as a device for spreading animals out, for the good of the whole species. We saw in chapter 4 that such group-selectionist arguments are not tenable. We have now also seen that the selection pressures that drive individuals to hold the territories they do may quite often include female choice as well as the need to command resources.

Promiscuity, polygyny, pair-bonding and polyandry

We have considered how animals (usually females) choose their mates. But what sorts of relationship do they form once they have found mates? In some cases the two animals may never see each other again once copulation has occurred; in others, they will stay together for the rest of their lives, rearing young together in breeding season after breeding season. Obviously these different kinds of relationships have profound implications for social structure.

Ethologists have borrowed terms from anthropology to describe most of the possibilities (I shall return to the significance of this borrowing in chapter 7). There is, however, no real name for the situation where animals are basically solitary, meet only for mating and lose contact immediately afterwards – but then, that does not really constitute a structured society at all. Such mating-only relationships are normal when there is no parental care, as in fish like the cod, but they do also occur in some cases where the female (e.g. most species of cat) or the male (e.g. the stickleback or Siamese fighting fish) looks after the young for an extended period.

Where there are more permanent groupings, we may find a situation where, whenever a female is in breeding condition, she will mate with any and all males who are available. This is what happens, for example, in chimpanzees. Females come into oestrus rather rarely (every two or three years), but when one does, almost all the adult males in the loose-knit social group will copulate with her, except her sons. They will not attempt to interfere with one another's matings (though juveniles, especially the female's dependent offspring, will). Perhaps because of the selective pressures this kind of mating system produces, male chimpanzees have extremely large testicles and extremely rapid ejaculation. This kind of mating system is called 'promiscuity'. It is usually associated with care of the young lying exclusively with the females, though the males may show a general tolerance towards juveniles.

Another mating system that sometimes looks like promiscuity, but is in fact somewhat different, is 'polygyny'. Here one male has exclusive access to a group (or 'harem') of females, or a small group of males share exclusive access to a larger group of females. The red deer is a good example of the first type of polygyny, and lions of the second kind. A common characteristic of polygynous species is that males tend to be bigger than females, and often quite different in appearance (red deer and lions both fit this well). As in promiscuous societies, care of the young is typically wholly female. Even male tolerance of young is not to be relied upon, especially if harems may change hands – remember the infanticidal lions and langurs.

A rare variant of polygyny occurs in English foxes. MacDonald (1979) showed that a group of related vixens associate with a single dog fox. The unusual feature is that only one or two of the females produce cubs, though all help to bring in food for the cubs.

Another common mating system, especially among birds, is pair-bonding, where one male and one female mate exclusively (or more or less exclusively) with each other. Pairs may be formed for one breeding season or for many. It is common, though not universal, for both members of a pair to play a substantial part in care of the offspring. Often, though, the female does more than the male, and sometimes they take different roles – for example, the male may build the nest, while the female does all the sitting. In hornbills, the male walls the female up in the nest (a hole in a tree), and then brings food to her. Males and females of pair-bonding species are usually rather similar in size and often, though not always, very similar in appearance.

Proceeding on a continuum from polygyny through pair-bonding, the natural point to arrive at is one where a single female has exclusive access to several mates. This is called 'polyandry'. Two different versions of polyandry have been described. One version involves the female taking the role more usually occupied by the male. This is what happens in the American jaçana, the polyandrous bird we met in chapter 4; like many male animals, the female jaçana holds a large territory, within which several males defend smaller territories against each other, build nests, hatch the eggs the female lays in them and care for the young. The female may, at most, help one of the males in parental care. In several physiological respects, too, the jaçana shows gender reversal: the female is almost twice as large as the male, it is the male rather than the female that has a brood patch to facilitate incubation and the female lays a large number of very small eggs (Jenni, 1974).

The second kind of polyandry does not involve role reversal. Faaborg and Patterson (1981) call it 'co-operative polyandry': a group of males all mate with a single female, and all assist in rearing the young. In the best-studied example, the Tasmanian native hen, the males are all brothers, and one of them mates much more often than the others. In the Galapagos hawk, however, unrelated groups of males share a mate, and in this case all mate equally often.

Neither kind of polyandry is particularly common. Both are important, though, for the light they throw on more typical mating systems. The jaçana's system is obviously the mirror image of the widespread 'nested territory' system of polygyny; co-operative polyandry is the mirror image of the system found in foxes, where only one vixen of a polygynous group breeds.

Sex roles, resources and parental care

As I have described the various mating systems, I have mentioned that they are associated with different patterns of parental care. Other factors also influence how the offspring will be cared for, of course: it makes a great difference whether the females in a harem are a matriline, for example, rather than an unrelated group; and the richness of the resources available in the environment must influence the extent of parental care that is necessary. How do these various factors fit together?

A few points are obvious. Fathers cannot be very closely involved in the care of their offspring in a promiscuous society, where they cannot know which offspring are theirs (though they may contribute to the welfare of the entire group, for example by alarm-calling). In most polygynous societies, fathers cannot contribute much parental care, because they would not have time (and the same is true for mothers in the jaçana type of polyandry). These kinds of society are obviously only viable in a relatively rich environment, where one adult is sufficient to find food for the young (and total absence of parental care, as in fish like the cod, obviously requires even more favourable ecological conditions).

But there are still questions to be asked. When one parent is sufficient to care for the young, why do we usually find polygyny rather than reversed-role polyandry? If the parents meet only to mate, why is it nearly always the mother rather than the father who cares for the young? When two adults are needed, why do we usually find mated pairs rearing their own young, rather than promiscuous groups with all males helping all females to rear the young? In the rare cases where more than two adults are needed, why do we more often find a polyandrous group as in the

Tasmanian native hen or the Galapagos hawk, rather than a polygynous group with only one female breeding, as in the fox? The prime key to these questions is the fact of anisogamy; a subsidiary one is that females can be more sure of their parenthood than males. Let us see how these factors work out.

Consider first the case where parents meet only to mate and separate immediately afterwards. In birds and mammals, fertilization is internal: the pressures derived from anisogamy have given the female physiological adaptations for feeding the new organism after fertilization, so that any parental care that goes beyond the physiologically imposed minimum is also going to be provided by the female – the male will already have left. Such females have lost what Dawkins (1976) calls the 'race to desert' the offspring long ago, in their evolutionary past. Where fertilization is external, as in fish, matters are more finely balanced, especially as males can be sure of their paternity and so their incentive to desert is reduced. Males cannot release their sperm into the water until the eggs have been released, and this gives the female an opportunity to leave. Accordingly, we find several species of fish where the males build nests, induce females to lay eggs in them, then fertilize the eggs and care for them until they hatch, and sometimes also care for the fry after hatching. The stickleback is one example (we considered its courtship in chapter 3), and another is the Siamese fighting fish, which builds a raft of bubbles as a nest on the surface of the water. Thus the pressures of anisogamy can be circumvented.

Once it becomes true within a species that one sex looks after the young exclusively, other adaptations to that fact may of course emerge. Male sticklebacks do not behave as though they are running a race to desert the young, in fact they chase the female away as soon as they have fertilized her eggs. Just as the female mammal is locked into providing maternal care far more obviously by the adaptations of gestation and lactation than by the underlying fact of anisogamy that originally favoured them, so the male stickleback is locked into providing paternal care, and that fact favours further adaptations which further confirm him in that role. By the time he mates, the male stickleback (or the male American jaçana) has committed considerable time and energy to establishing and defending a territory, and building a nest on it: he could not afford to abandon the fertilized eggs to the doubtful care of the female and start to hunt for a new territory.

The formation of harems and other polygynous relationships is another example of an adaptation to a pre-existing sex role. Most hoofed animals live in environments where one adult can look after the young (which are in any case born in a relatively highly developed state). Since they are mammals, care of the young therefore falls to the females, and this fact makes the females a valuable resource which it is to the males' advantage to fight over before they are in full breeding condition, and to defend until they reach it.

Where two adults are required to care for the young, simple relationship factors will determine that the society will usually consist of mated pairs of adults caring for their own young, rather than a commune with all males and all females contributing to the care of all young. Adults that cared for all young indiscriminately would be systematically outbred by those that concentrated on the young that carried their own genes.

Granting that it will usually be parents who look after their own young, why do we so often find the formation of a strong pair bond, with all the signalling instincts involved in bond formation and the subsequent maintenance of the relationship? If both parents are going to contribute to looking after the young, both are under strong selective pressures concerning pair formation. Any behaviour that helps a female find a mate who really will stay around and help rear the young will confer a selective advantage on her – this is especially so where there is some chance that a female alone could rear at least some young, so that the male is under some pressure to desert. Any behaviour that ensures that the young a male is supporting really are his own offspring will be advantageous to him. Indulging for a moment in armchair adaptationism, we can also see that there will be some selective pressure on females to mate with males other than their own partners, if they can do so undetected by their mates, since the sons of such successful 'adulterers' will presumably also tend to be successfully adulterous. And there will be a pressure on males to mate with females paired with other males, again if they can do so undetected, since they will then have offspring reared for them by the other male.

Of course, all these tendencies are to be put into effect by instincts (which is just as well – with so many costs and benefits to calculate, who would be a garden bird?). It is no wonder that the instincts associated with pair formation and maintenance are so complex. A few general trends may be picked out, however.

First, it is common for the males of pair-bonding species to secure a territory, and often to build one or several nests on it, before acquiring a mate. The advantage to the female of postponing mate choice in this way is obvious. The male's contribution to care of the young is already half made before she chooses him, and not only does that ensure that he cannot desert without making it, it also reduces the chance that he will desert subsequently – since it will cost him a substantial amount of time and energy to get back to the same position again (though this will work only if all females in the species refuse to take males who have no nests to offer).

Secondly, where lengthy pair relationships occur, the courtship rituals of the two sexes tend to be symmetrical. No doubt this is partly a function of the fact that in strongly pair-bonding species male and female often look alike (though it could also be a cause of that fact). But there is also an underlying selective pressure: since both male and female are committing substantial resources to the mating, both need to be sure that they are mating with an individual of the right species. To some extent, anisogamy is being overlaid by the equal commitment of time the parents will have to make to the young after fertilization.

In general, however, anisogamy has pervasive effects. There is no sudden leap from environments where one adult can rear up young to environments where two are needed. Where the care of one parent and a bit is required, it is nearly always the female who provides the one and the male who provides the bit: sitting on eggs for fewer hours, bringing in less food for fledglings, deserting when the young are almost but not quite independent. Although there are exceptions, as we have seen, parental care in the animal kingdom predominantly does mean maternal care.

The nature of parental care

As we have seen, parental care is often necessary if the young are to survive. But in what form is it provided?

Chapters 2 and 3 included many examples of the instincts that subserve parental care. Both parents and young have these instincts. Young blue tits instinctively gape when parents arrive at their nests; parent blue tits instinctively put food into gaping orange throats. Herring-gull chicks instinctively beg at objects that are red and have light/dark boundaries; parent herring gulls instinctively disgorge food when their yellow-and-red bills are pecked at. Human babies instinctively turn their heads towards objects that touch their cheeks; human mothers, perhaps instinctively and perhaps not, put their nipples to the mouth of a baby that turns towards them. It is obvious why there should be so many instinctive behaviour patterns concerned with the interactions of parents and young. The newborn mammal or newly hatched chick has had no opportunity to learn what to do, and needs to 'know instinctively'. The parents may never have produced young before, and may never be going to do so again: they too cannot afford to learn everything from experience.

Even so, not all interactions between parents and young are subserved by simple instincts. A much discussed example of a more complex process occurs in species where the young are able to move around from the moment they are born or hatched. When such animals live in groups, both parents and young are faced with the problem of recognizing each other. As we have already seen, there is a selective pressure on parents to care only for their own young, and this creates a selective pressure on the offspring to approach only their own parents. Even where such animals are solitary, the young need to keep in touch with their parents.

In such species, there is a rapid kind of learning that is predisposed to happen at the time of birth or hatching. Lorenz first discovered this in his greylag geese: a gander which he had hand-reared came to follow him everywhere, and when it reached sexual maturity it attempted to mate with him. In other words, it treated him in all respects as though he was a mother goose. Lorenz called this kind of learning 'imprinting'.

What seems to happen, at least in ducks, geese and chickens, is this. The young bird is predisposed to learn the characteristics of any object that it sees and hears during a fairly short period soon after hatching, nowadays referred to as the 'sensitive period'. Normally, what the young bird will see and hear during the sensitive period is its mother. But if we arrange things so that what it sees is Konrad Lorenz, or a red watering-can, or a blue flashing light borrowed from a police car, then it will learn the characteristics of that object instead. Bright, coloured, noisy, moving objects are the most effective stimuli for imprinting experiments. But if no such stimuli are available, then chicks will even imprint on their own feet.

Although imprinting is most often studied in ducks and chickens, it occurs in many other species. For example an imprinting process has been held to underlie mutual recognition by nanny goats and their kids. Unless a goat is able to see and smell her kid very shortly after birth, she will subsequently refuse to suckle it (Klopfer, Adams and Klopfer, 1964). Although it has recently been suggested that the mother may take an active role by marking the kid in some way (Gubernick, Jones and Klopfer, 1979), there is obviously a sensitive period here, whatever the mechanism. It has also been suggested that imprinting processes may be involved in the formation of bonds between human mothers and their babies – this is discussed in chapter 6.

Why is imprinting so common? As we saw, much about the relations between parents and young can be left to instinct. It is not hard to imagine a genetically determined mechanism that would ensure that a herring-gull chick will peck at red, contoured objects. It is less obvious how the genes could tell a gosling which one of numerous mother geese it should follow. What nature seems to give the gosling is the 'knowledge' that it will have a mother, and that it should respond to her by following her. It does not tell it what she will look like. Instinct gives the chick a concept of mother, but the environment has to supply the details.

To a psychologist, that looks very like a biological version of a Jungian archetype. Jung (1917/1966) supposed that we have a 'collective unconscious', a common inheritance of behavioural tendencies and possible social roles, or archetypes, that influence our behaviour but do not come into our awareness. Scientific psychologists have often dismissed this idea, but it is not really implausible if we remember that we are descended from creatures whose social behaviour was determined by processes like instinct and imprinting, and that at least the residues of these processes remain with us today. A human baby will respond selectively to his or her own mother's bra pads by 3 days of age (MacFarlane, 1975), and to her voice by 30 days at the latest (Mehler, Bertoncini, Barrière and Jassik-Gerschenfeld, 1978). It may well turn out that imprinting-like processes are involved in this rapid learning, though we should bear in mind that ours is not a species in which the young are mobile immediately on birth – quite the opposite.

The necessity of parental care

Instincts and imprinting mediate parental care. But how essential is that care? In many cases, if parental care is withdrawn, or even if one member of a bonded pair is lost, the young will simply die of starvation, cold or predation. If, in laboratory conditions, we prevent that happening, deleterious consequences may follow at the psychological level. In a famous series of experiments, Harlow and Harlow (e.g. 1965) showed that rhesus monkey infants reared in total isolation behaved very strangely, and when they grew to adulthood they were seriously impaired: neither males nor females would mate normally (males were interested in females but incompetent, while females refused to accept males). If the females were forcibly inseminated they were unable to care for their young. There was also some tendency to excessive aggressiveness. Even short periods of separation from their mothers can affect the development of young rhesus monkeys, though how serious the effect is depends on the nature of the mother–infant relationship before separation (Hinde and Spencer-Booth, 1971). Extreme consequences can follow the death of a primate mother. Jane Van Lawick-Goodall (1974) records what happened after the death of Flo, one of the chimpanzee mothers she studied at the Gombe Stream reserve in Tanzania. Flo's 8-year-old son Flint, who was almost fully grown and foraged entirely for himself, became listless, stopped eating and died within a fortnight. What he suffered sounds very much like human depression (something that Suomi and Harlow, 1972, have claimed to be able to model by subjecting rhesus monkeys to isolation and sensory deprivation), and it is significant that the best-understood cause of depression in humans is bereavement.

Much has been made of these results, especially the Harlows', and they have been used to support the idea that a bond with a single mother figure is essential for healthy development in human children. But this is drawing far too much from the data. First, in subsequent experiments, Harlow and his collaborators have shown that infants reared with their mothers, but without other infants, behaved normally when young but grew into disturbed adults. Young monkeys reared without their mothers, but with other infants, behaved very oddly as infants but grew into normal adults. Thus, in the rhesus monkey at least, it is peer deprivation rather than maternal deprivation that does long-term damage. Secondly, there are many animals, including some primates, where care of the young is a less exclusively female matter than it is in the rhesus monkey or chimpanzee. Why should we assume that the rhesus monkey provides the best model for the consequences of maternal deprivation in humans?

Non-maternal care

We have already seen that, though parental care most often comes from the mother, at least some contribution from the father is to be expected in any pair-bonding species. We have also encountered species, such as the jaçana and the stickleback, where parental care is exclusively male. Mitchell (1969) has reviewed the extent of paternal care in primates, and his data are obviously relevant to any debate over what sex roles are natural for human beings. In several pair-bonding New World primates, such as the titi and some of the marmosets, the male carries the infants most of the time they are not actually suckling. This is extreme. More typical, perhaps, is the situation of the Japanese monkey, which has a well-defined breeding season. The females provide most of the care for the young during their first year, but when a new infant is born, the males take on some of the care of the yearlings, tending to carry them about, remove them from danger, and so forth.

It is not only parents that care for young animals. Among troop-living primates, a very common phenomenon is what is known as 'aunting' (e.g. Rowell, Hinde and Spencer-Booth, 1964). A newborn infant is an object of intense interest to juvenile females who have not yet given birth themselves. If the mother permits it, these females will pick the infant up, pass it from one to other, even run off with it. Bearing in mind the effects of total isolation on subsequent maternal competence, as revealed in the Harlows' experiments, it is very probable that this 'aunting' experience is important in teaching the young females how to react when in due course they have infants themselves. But why should the mothers permit it? Infants in inexperienced hands are in some danger. Partly, perhaps, the 'aunts' give the mother some rest – infant monkeys normally spend most of their time clinging to their mothers' fur. But it is also probable that the aunts will be related to the mother. If the experience raises their chances of

83

being successful mothers, that will be to the present mother's genetic advantage. Aunting may thus be maintained by kin selection.

Another case where individuals other than the parents have a role in rearing the young is the much studied one of 'helpers at the nest' in birds. In some species of birds that lay more than one clutch of eggs each year, such as moorhens, the young of the first brood stay with their parents throughout the summer and help to bring food for the second brood. This is of course readily understood in terms of kin selection. The second brood will be full siblings to the first: from the point of view of gene content, helping to rear them will be as good for the first brood as rearing young of their own, which they are in any case not yet mature enough to do.

The most extreme case of 'parental' care by non-parents is the situation in eusocial insects such as bees, where sterile workers do all the work of rearing their sisters. A great deal of discussion has been devoted to the evolution of eusociality. Some of the issues are too technical to go into here. It is worth noting, though, that because of the chromosomal make-up of Hymenoptera, bees are more closely related to their sisters than is the case in vertebrates.

Parent–offspring conflict

So far, I have taken it for granted that parents will have an interest in caring for their young. Obviously, unless the young survive, the parents' genes are doomed to extinction. None the less, we find a very wide range of quantity and quality of parental care in animal species, ranging from the codfish which abandons its young as soon as they are fertilized, to human beings who provide for their young for nine months before birth and many years after it. What determines how much parental care will be shown, and what brings it to a halt at the appropriate point in each species?

Obviously there must be an inverse relationship between the number of young produced and the amount of care they are given. For any environment, there is an optimum number of young for parents to produce. Where a species is invading a new environment, the advantage lies in large numbers of young and little parental care for each of them. Where everything is more or less stable, and the emphasis is on competition between finely matched individuals for strictly limited resources, the parents' advantage lies in pouring resources into a small number of offspring, to give them the best possible chance. Within these broad alternatives, the ideal number of young varies according to circumstances: in a harsh season, songbirds lay fewer eggs than usual, and those that lay more than average bring fewer chicks than average through to fledging (Lack, 1954). If food supplies take a turn for the worse, parents may stop feeding the weakest of a litter, eat it, or feed it to its siblings (Polis, 1981).

Subject to these constraints, though, the parents' interests are likely to lie in distributing food equally between the members of a brood. But, even in a litter which is of ideal size from the parents' perspective, each chick's interest will be in getting more than its fair share of the available food. To be sure, each chick has an interest in its siblings' survival: they share half its genes, and so are as good as offspring for it. (We can see how important this factor is when we consider what happens when it is absent, as when a baby cuckoo hatches out in a songbird's nest.) But the chick has a stronger interest in its own survival than in its siblings' survival. Thus each chick is likely to be adapted to demand more food than the parent is likely to be adapted to give: there is a conflict of interest between parent and offspring (Trivers, 1974). Clearly this selective pressure will tend to exaggerate the signalling instincts by which chicks release food presentation in their parents; it may also explain the difference between the craning, gaping, begging display of the ten or so chicks in a blue tit nest and the relatively decorous begging peck of the two or three chicks of the herring gull.

Parent–offspring conflict can also occur when only one offspring is born at a time. Here the focus of the conflict is the point at which the offspring should become independent. When the young is just born or hatched, its interests and its parents' both demand that the parents should support it. When the young animal is fully grown, its genetic interests are not served by letting the parents support it – it would be better for them to be rearing new offspring, which would after all be siblings. In between, however, there is a stage of conflict, when the parents' best interests lie in abandoning the present offspring and producing a new one, while the offspring will have more young of its own, over its lifetime, if the parents continue to care for it. The theory of parent–offspring conflict is well worked out, but we do not have much satisfactory empirical data on it. Part of the problem is that, as with the 'race to desert the young', animals that are involved in parent–offspring conflict may not appear to be conflicting until we examine the costs and benefits of their behaviour quite closely. Also, comparative psychologists working with primates have tended to look for evidence of the kind of parent–offspring conflict that troubles modern western human societies, namely young people seeking independence before their parents are ready to grant it. Our present, sociobiological approach suggests this emphasis may be misplaced. The only really obvious example of parent–offspring conflict concerns weaning: many mammals wean their young more or less forcibly.

Human sex and parent roles

Almost every paragraph of this chapter has been rich in potential implications for human life. The very vocabulary of mating systems is borrowed from the description of human societies, and the literature of sociobiology is rich in other borrowings. I have tried to avoid the more contentious of these (descriptions of forced copulation in non-humans as 'rape', for example, have been heavily criticized, e.g. by Gowaty, 1982), though there is no doubt that they can add colour and provoke thought. But concepts like imprinting, paternal care, parent–offspring conflict shout out to be applied to human affairs, at least to see whether or not they fit. Chapter 7 will be devoted to discussing what conclusions we can properly draw from animal behaviour that are applicable to human affairs. But at this point it is worth isolating three major themes.

First, both in the relations between the sexes and in the relations between parents and young, we have identified selective pressures which are different for the different partners in the relationship and will tend to drive them into conflict with each other. This is important, because it is easy to think that harmonious relationships are the only natural ones. This is not so. In so far as our genes influence our behaviour, we should expect them to lead us into conflict with those with whom we share our lives.

Secondly, the environment has a paramount influence on social structure. We have seen that already in chapter 4; in this chapter it has emerged as a crucial determinant of mating systems. The implication is obvious. Where closely related species of animals live in environments of very different severity, they may have very different social structures; and so it proves. One of the many ways in which human beings are unusual is the very wide range of environments, virtually from equator to pole, which we can inhabit. It follows that we may expect humans to show a very wide range of social structures, and so we do.

Finally, although there are many aspects of mating and parenting that are well served by instincts, we also find that learning has an essential role to play. We discussed the way in which parents and young learn to recognize each other; we could equally well have spent time on the learning processes which the members of a pair bond must undergo. An account of animal behaviour that focused only on demonstrable instincts and theoretically inevitable evolutionary tendencies would be radically incomplete, and grossly unsuitable to be applied to the human case. It is time to turn our attention to learning.

6

Learning, intelligence and culture

Not everything that animals do can be accounted for in terms of instinct. Any creature that finds food, or a nest, or a mate more quickly and efficiently on a second trial than a first is profiting from its ability to learn. Psychologists have been submitting animals' learning capacities to systematic analysis for nearly a hundred years. We shall use some of their results in this chapter, but our emphasis will not be where the comparative psychologists have put it. Their concern has been to abstract learning from any particular biological context, so as to study its most general laws. Our concern here is to see how learning fits into a biological context.

What and why do animals learn?

Psychologists studying animal learning have identified a number of simple experimental procedures in which learning can be demonstrated in any arbitrarily chosen animal. These procedures show some of the kinds of information that animals can learn.

The simplest of all learning procedures is called 'habituation'. This can be carried out with any stimulus that will elicit a response from an animal, including, for example, Lorenzian releasers. If the stimulus is presented repeatedly, the response it elicits will wane and eventually disappear. This is not due to simple tiring out either of the perceptual apparatus or of the muscles making the response, for if a slightly different stimulus is presented, the response will return in full force. Habituation is a specific reduction in the capacity of a particular stimulus to elicit a particular response. Its occurrence shows that animals can learn to recognize stimuli. Indeed, it is often used as a research tool when it is in doubt whether particular stimuli can be recognized. For example, Catriona Ryan (1982) investigated whether pigeons could recognize other individuals of the same species, by recording the frequency of the bowing fixed action pattern elicited when she put an object pigeon next to the cage of a subject pigeon. After five or six five-minute trials, the subject ceased to bow when the object was presented; but when it was replaced by a second object bird, indistinguishable from the first to the human eye, the subject's bowing promptly reappeared.

The next procedure in order of simplicity is called 'classical' or 'Pavlovian conditioning'. As almost everyone knows, Pavlov (e.g. 1927) found that if he repeatedly rang a bell (or operated a metronome, or sounded a tuning fork, or flashed a light, or made a *blub-blub-blub* sound by bubbling air through water – Pavlov's experimental procedures have a certain period charm) just before feeding a dog, the dog soon came to salivate as soon as the bell (or whatever) was sounded. Pavlovian conditioning has been studied in enormous detail in a wide variety of species; its importance for us, however, is simply that it shows that animals can learn to use one stimulus as a predictor of the occurrence of another. It is predictiveness rather than mere co-occurrence that is required if Pavlovian conditioning is to take place. This is shown by the observations that response to the bell alone is much weakened if the bell is followed by food only on some randomly selected trials, or if the food is frequently presented without first sounding the bell (a relatively recent discovery: Rescorla, 1967).

The final kind of simple learning procedure is called 'instrumental' or 'operant conditioning'. It was used in the earliest animal learning experiments, for example when W.S. Small

(1900–1) taught rats to run through a scaled-down model of the Hampton Court maze to find a food reward in the centre, or E.L. Thorndike (1898) rewarded cats with food for escaping from puzzle boxes. But it was brought to prominence in the 1930s most especially by B.F. Skinner. In his famous box, Skinner (1938) arranged that every time a rat pressed a small lever, a pellet of food would be delivered. Skinner's contribution was not so much to show that rats could learn ways of getting food, no news to the species on which rats have been parasites for thousands of years, as to invent a situation in which this apparently intelligent, purposive activity could be subjected to systematic analysis and be shown to have laws at least as reliable as those of habituation or Pavlovian conditioning. From our point of view, the importance of operant conditioning is that it shows that animals can learn what responses produce particular outcomes. There has been much dispute as to exactly what kinds of stimuli will serve as effective rewards when presented after a response (stimuli which have this property are called 'reinforcers'). We do not need to solve that problem here, but it is worth noting that, so far as is known, any Lorenzian sign stimulus will be a reinforcer under the right conditions. Obviously food and water, which trigger off eating and drinking, are reinforcers, but so also, for example, is the presentation of a rival, which releases aggressive display, to an aggressive animal like a fighting cock, stickleback or Siamese fighting fish, (e.g. Thompson, 1963).

There are many kinds of learning that cannot easily be assimilated to these simple models; imitation is an obvious example. In any case, many animal psychologists now believe that animals in both classical and instrumental conditioning are actually making use of complex cognitive capacities to solve the problem posed by the experiment (Dickinson, 1981). In this chapter, therefore, we shall not use simple conditioning to 'explain away' other kinds of learning.

From the literature on habituation and conditioning, we can see that animals are very ready to learn about biologically relevant stimuli. Habituation can only be studied if we start with a stimulus that elicits a definite response, and the same is true of classical conditioning. Sign stimuli are the obvious choice. Instrumental conditioning depends on our finding a suitable reinforcer, and we have seen that these too are often sign stimuli. This is not to say that learning about arbitrary 'neutral' stimuli is impossible – it may just be difficult to demonstrate. But we can conclude that anything relevant to an animal's instincts is likely to be good raw material for learning. This should modify any idea that instincts are inflexible components of animal behaviour; it should also modify any idea that learning creates a means of determining behaviour that is totally divorced from instinct.

Foraging and learning

What are sometimes called the 'laws of learning' have largely been worked out by psychologists studying the behaviour of animals searching for food rewards or reacting to food presented unconditionally. Is there anything in animals' natural life to which we can relate this body of laboratory experimentation?

Animals in the wild have to find food just as much as animals in psychological laboratories do. In recent years, behavioural ecologists have been studying the natural food-gathering behaviours of animals in considerable detail, and it is becoming clear that the analogy between natural foraging and conditioning experiments is real and useful.

Much of the ecological literature on foraging has focused on the idea that the pressures of natural selection will tend to turn animals into optimal foragers, who extract food from their environment in the best possible way (MacArthur and Pianka, 1966). If conditions are well enough defined, it is possible to work out mathematically what the optimal forager should do, and so we can compare the behaviour of real foragers with various optimal models. For example, if an optimal forager is faced with two kinds of prey, both of which it encounters occasionally as it moves through its habitat, it should obviously take the better type whenever it finds it. But the probability of taking the worse type should vary, and it should depend on the frequency with which the *better* type is found, not on its own frequency at all. Goss-Custard (1977) watched redshank feeding in the mud of English estuaries, and found that they took two kinds of prey: a crustacean, *Corophium*, and polychaete worms. *Corophium* was always taken, whenever found, but the probability that worms would be taken depended strongly on the frequency at which the bird was finding *Corophium*, and only weakly on the frequency of worms. Redshank are therefore almost, though not quite, optimal foragers.

This kind of optimal model relies to a considerable extent on the forager's instincts. The redshank may well 'know' instinctively that *Corophia* are better prey than worms. But there must also be some element of learning. Instinct cannot tell the redshank how frequent crustaceans and worms will be on a particular stretch of beach. To emphasize the role of learning in foraging, I repeated Goss-Custard's procedures, using pigeons in an ordinary laboratory Skinner box and mimicking prey densities with the kind of 'schedules of reinforcement' devised by Skinner as rules for reinforcing some but not all instrumental responses (Lea, 1979). I obtained results very similar to Goss-Custard's, and similar results have been obtained using rats (Collier and Rovee-Collier, 1981).

The most recent approaches to optimal foraging put even more stress on learning. Krebs, Kacelnik and Taylor (1978) considered the problem of a forager faced with two 'patches' in its environment. The forager knows that both patches are the sort of place where food should be found, but does not know the density of food in either patch. Krebs and his colleagues showed that the optimal forager should at first divide its time equally between the two patches, until one of them has clearly yielded more prey than the other, at which point it should remain in the better patch. Krebs, Kacelnik and Taylor arranged an experiment in which great tits obtained food by hopping on to either of two perches. In effect, this was an operant conditioning procedure, with two different responses available. Hops on the two perches had different probabilities of giving food, so they were like 'patches' of different densities. As optimal foraging theory predicts, the great tits at first sampled both perches ('patches'), but by the end of a session hopped consistently on the one that was more likely to yield food. Furthermore, the optimal forager should spend longer switching between patches the longer it has available to spend in the environment. In experiments that are yet to be published, Alex Kacelnik and Susan Dow have claimed that great tits and pigeons will do this, though the effect is not strong.

The kinds of learning studied in conditioning experiments may well have evolved under the selective pressure of the need to forage optimally (Lea, 1981). Foraging is a sufficiently widespread and general activity of animals to have produced the widespread and general learning principles that seem to be uncovered by the psychologists' experiments on learning.

Biological boundaries of learning theory

None the less, more complex and specialized kinds of learning are also involved in foraging. An example is the remarkable capacity of marsh tits and nutcrackers to remember where they have hidden nuts and seeds (Shettleworth, 1983). Traditional 'learning theory' is certainly not completely general: the so-called laws of learning do not apply to every situation, and cannot be applied without regard for the adaptive significance of the kinds of behaviour involved.

The clearest demonstration of this comes in an experiment on the way in which rats avoid painful and dangerous stimuli. Wild rats learn very readily to avoid poisonous substances: survivors of a poisoning attempt become 'bait-shy' and are unlikely to be killed unless the poison or the bait is changed (Chitty, 1954, p. 278 ff.). From the point of view of learning theory, this is rather odd, since poisoning does not usually cause illness until hours after the food has been taken, while in conditioning experiments, reinforcers usually lose their effectiveness if they are delayed by even a few minutes or seconds (Tarpy and Sawabini, 1974).

Garcia and Koelling (1966) carried out an experiment to contrast the two situations more precisely. While drinking from a water tube, rats were exposed to one of two kinds of harmless cue stimulus. One group of rats received a sudden sweet taste (saccharin was put in the water). The other group of rats saw a bright light and heard a distinctive noise whenever they licked the tube. Three hours later, the rats were hurt in one of two ways. Half of each group was given a brief electric shock. The other half of each group was exposed to a dose of X-rays sufficient to make the recipients ill. To test what the rats had learned, they were later allowed access to the water tube, with either the sweet taste or the audio-visual cue again present. The rats that had been shocked after a sweet taste drank sweet water as though nothing had happened, and those that had been nauseated after drinking 'bright and noisy' water drank freely in the presence of these audio-visual cues. These rats had clearly learned nothing. But the rats that had received a shock after the audio-visual cue, and especially those that had been made ill after the sweet taste, virtually refused to drink. These two groups had clearly learned that the cues signalled danger.

How should we interpret these results? What made the difference between learning and not learning was the *combination* of cues with unpleasant events. Taste and illness seem to belong together, and so do external (audio-visual) cues and externally applied pain (electric shock). These combinations make biological sense. A rat that avoided everything it had seen and heard in the hours before becoming ill would not survive as long as one that avoided what it had tasted in that time.

There are several other known instances where biologically relevant combinations lead to especially effective learning. We saw in chapter 2 how Shettleworth (1975) was able to teach hamsters to rear up, or dig, or scrabble for food reward, but not to scratch, wash or scent-mark. Seligman (1970) has suggested that biologically relevant combinations lead not just to faster learning but to special kinds of learning. He suggests that associations between stimuli (or between responses and stimuli) fall into three classes, prepared, unprepared and contraprepared, and that different laws of learning apply to each class. Associations between tastes and illness would be, for a rat, prepared, because they are biologically useful. Associations between the bar of a Skinner box and food would be unprepared, because evolution knows nothing of Skinner boxes, one way or the other. The association between scratching and food for a hamster, though, would be contraprepared, because it is a biological nonsense – it involves stimuli related to two quite different drive systems. Seligman (1971) argues that people are biologically prepared to learn associations between fear and such stimuli as snakes, spiders and heights; and that this is why people often suffer from phobias to such things, but rarely to apparently equally frightening modern artefacts such as vacuum cleaners or firearms.

The proposed distinct laws of Seligman's three kinds of association have never emerged from the experimental literature. However, it certainly is true that many animals show special kinds of learning which do not fit into the pattern of general laws of learning derived from conditioning experiments. My own view is that conditioning procedures usually tap into general learning processes which probably evolved to allow optimal foraging. They would therefore be expected to be very similar in all animals, since all animals must forage. But the various special kinds of learning have probably evolved separately for each species or group that possesses them, and so each should be expected to have its own distinct laws. Let us look at some of these special kinds of learning.

Special learning abilities

One of the best known of the special learning abilities is imprinting, which we considered briefly in chapter 5: the rapid learning of (usually) the mother's appearance by newly hatched chicks. There has been much argument among psychologists and ethologists as to whether imprinting is, or is not, a special kind of learning. It certainly does not involve the procedures of either classical or instrumental conditioning. Lorenz (1935/1970b) argued that it must involve a special process, distinct from ordinary learning, since it was exceptionally fast, was irreversible and could only occur within a sharply defined critical period. But the concept of a critical period has been replaced by that of a more loosely specified sensitive period: imprinting is most likely to occur within the sensitive period, but can occur outside it. Recent experiments have shown, too, that imprinting can sometimes be reversed. And though imprinting is certainly a rapid kind of learning, this can reasonably be explained by the fact that the animal concerned has had virtually no previous learning experience, and so there is no scope for what learning psychologists call 'proactive interference' from previous tasks.

But if imprinting probably does not involve any special process, its occurrence in specific contexts does seem to involve specific adaptations to each species' particular mode of life. We have already considered imprinting in birds and in mutual recognition by nanny-goats and kids. Another example, interesting because it does not involve a social behaviour, occurs in fish of the salmon type. Thunburg (1971) studied it in the alewife, which breeds in the rivers that flow to the Atlantic coast of North America. Juvenile alewives leave their natal rivers and live in the sea until the time comes for them to breed, when they always return to the river in which they were themselves spawned. Thunburg showed that alewives discriminate their natal streams by the traces of chemicals present in the water, and they must learn this during the relatively brief period they spend in the rivers after hatching.

A second special kind of learning is the acquisition of song by birds (Konishi and Nottebohm, 1969). In some species it has been claimed that song is completely instinctive: song sparrows hatched and reared by canaries in sound-proof rooms grow up to sing completely normally. More usually, song can be shown to be at least partly learned. There are two types of evidence for this. First, in most species, birds raised in acoustic isolation sing abnormally or not at all. Young male chaffinches usually begin by singing what is called 'subsong' – snatches and elements of the full chaffinch song. Birds that have no opportunity to hear male chaffinches singing while they are nestlings never develop beyond the subsong stage. Notice the special features of the learning involved here: at the nestling stage, chaffinches do not sing at all, yet experience at this time, when it could not be reflected in behaviour, is of profound importance. Very extensive song-learning is possible – individual marsh wrens may have as many as a hundred songs (Kroodsma, 1977). The second kind of evidence that song is learned comes from studies of 'local dialects' in bird song (Thielcke, 1969). Typically, the songs of individuals of a species that live near one another are more alike than the songs of more widely separated birds. By moving eggs from one nest to another, it can be shown that these geographical variations do not have a genetic basis. Thus local groups of birds have their own culturally transmitted variant of the species' song. Indeed, in so far as bird song is learned, it always constitutes a simple form of culture: its continuance depends on the young in each generation learning from the behaviour of their parents.

Another very special set of learning abilities are those involved in the linked but distinct skills of migration and homing, both of which have been most studied in birds (Matthews, 1968) though both occur in other groups. In some species, migration seems to be completely instinctive. Young cuckoos, for example, must find their way from Britain to Africa in the autumn without guidance from their parents, whom they never meet. In other species (e.g. greylag geese) migration takes place in family parties or large groups and it is possible for learning to supplement or replace instinct in specifying the route to be taken. Perdeck (1958) showed that juvenile starlings displaced from their home area before the autumn migration set off in the compass direction characteristic of their home population, and so this direction must be specified instinctively. But adult starlings displaced in the same way set out in the right direction to reach the place where they had wintered in previous years: learning has obviously overlaid instinct. When we consider homing, learning is of course very strongly to the fore. The homing capacities of pigeons are famous, but in some ways they are exceeded by those of seabirds such as the Manx shearwater or Leach's petrel, which have been known to return to their nests within a fortnight of being removed to the wrong side of the Atlantic.

Human special learning abilities

Does our own species have any special learning abilities on a par with imprinting, song-learning or migration in birds? This question leads us into some controversial areas.

It has often been suggested that imprinting-like processes occur in the formation of the bond between human mothers and their newborn babies. If this is true, then babies who are removed to intensive or special care units at birth (as is routine practice when birth weight is low) may be at a disadvantage: a sensitive period for the formation of the bond with the mother may be missed. By the time the baby is discharged, either the mother or the baby may not be in the right condition for bond formation. It is certainly true that some mothers whose babies spend a substantial time in special care do report difficulties in forming a satisfying relationship with their babies. The modern tendency, at least in Britain, is to allow parents much freer access to special care units, and there is no doubt that this is worthwhile, if only for the relief it affords parents at the time (and I write here from the experience of having had a premature baby in special care for three months). But, while there may be slight peculiarities in the ways in which the mothers whose babies have been in special care interact with them, and these may persist for some time, there is no evidence that the bond between mother and baby is any less strong in general (Richards, 1979).

A second area where imprinting-like processes have been invoked to explain human learning is the acquisition of language. Perhaps, it is said, there is a sensitive period during which children are able to learn to talk; if they miss this period, either because they are deaf or because they are among those rare cases of children brought up out of all contact with speaking humans, language-learning becomes difficult or impossible.

The evidence in favour of a sensitive period for language acquisition is weak. The so-called 'wild children' (Malson, 1972) provide tantalizing, fascinating but fundamentally unreliable evidence. The circumstances in which they come to be isolated tend to be so odd, and their probable innate endowment with intelligence so low, that any deficiencies of learning they show once they are discovered would admit of a hundred and one explanations. All things considered, the fact that many of them do develop at least some language must be taken as evidence against the sensitive-period account of language-learning.

Much more plausible is the proposal that language involves a special human learning ability on a par with the pigeon's ability to learn to home or the marsh wren to learn songs. Some of the evidence needed to consider this question will be dealt with below, when we look at the various attempts to teach language-like behaviours to apes. But the idea receives at least some support from the fact that there are parts of the brain apparently concerned with language and no other function. Damage to certain parts of the brain may leave a person unable to speak or unable to understand speech, but otherwise apparently of unimpaired intelligence (Williams, 1979).

Chomsky (1957) suggested that the unique requirement for understanding language was a representation, within the mind, of the language's *generative grammar* – the finite set of rules that are capable of generating the infinite number of sentences that are grammatical within the language. On this argument, what makes humans unique must be an innate capacity to acquire an internalized generative grammar. Not everyone agrees that language-learning is a special kind of ability, however. Clowes (1971) suggested that the perception of objects may require exactly the same kind of internalized generative grammar as understanding language, and seeing things is something that we assume that other animals do as well as we do. Perhaps human evolution has simply adapted a general learning capacity (though not one we have considered so far) to special ends.

Before we can properly consider the special nature of human

learning capacities, however, we need to consider how much other animals actually can achieve. What are the limits of animal learning?

Animal intelligence

Considering the amount of experimental work there has been on animal learning, remarkably little of it has been devoted to pushing animals' intellects to their limits. Most of the experiments take the form of isolated *tours de force* rather than systematic explorations of well-defined areas.

One of the better explored areas is the establishment of complex response skills. One of Skinner's major contributions to psychology was his method of response-shaping, in which the experimenter starts with whatever behaviour an animal spontaneously shows, and rewards those aspects of it which seem most likely to lead in a desired direction. By sufficient small changes in the criterion for reward, the spectrum of behaviour is gradually shifted, until quite elaborate responses are established. Skinner (1962) once taught two pigeons to play a version of table tennis. Powell and Kelly (1975) used shaping to train a crow to use a 'tool'. A switch was placed out of reach of the bird's beak, behind some wire mesh. By starting with a rigid rod hung in line with the switch, and rewarding the bird whenever it touched this rod, Powell and Kelly eventually brought about a situation where the crow would pick up a cocktail stick from the Skinner box floor, hold it at just the right angle in its beak, and poke it through the wire so that it operated the switch.

Spontaneous tool-use also occurs in the animal kingdom. In some cases, it seems to be a very special, one-off adaptation to a particular ecological niche and may well be controlled by Lorenzian innate releasing mechanisms. An example is the woodpecker finch of the Galapagos islands. The islands have no true woodpeckers, but a species of finch lives off the prey that woodpeckers take elsewhere, probing into cracks and holes in tree bark by using a small stick. This foraging method is nothing like as efficient as using a stout beak, and it is presumably only absence of more specialized competitors in the isolated island ecology that has allowed it to evolve. Other cases are more equivocal: sea otters use stones to break open clams: is this a specialized IRM or an example of otter general learning ability? Chimpanzees seem to have a very general capacity to use tools, and are very readily taught to perform every kind of trick with them in captivity; in the wild, too, they have been observed to tear down branches to throw or shake at predatory leopards, to beat on old oil drums to frighten rivals, and to trim down twigs so that they can be used for fishing termites out of holes in their nests.

Another aspect of animal intelligence which has recently been studied systematically is the formation and use of complex concepts. Two kinds have been considered: abstract logical concepts like 'sameness' or 'symmetry', and complex percepts like 'a person' or 'a tree'. In either case the general technique is the same. An animal (usually a pigeon) is exposed to a series of instances and non-instances of the concept, and rewarded with food if it performs some response (usually pecking at a switch, called a key) in the presence of instances of the concept, but not if it responds to non-instances. Acquisition of the concept discrimination is later tested by giving the subject new instances and non-instances, not used in training, and seeing how it responds. The conclusions to be drawn for the case of abstract logical concepts are still in dispute. But in the case of complex perceptual concepts, there is little doubt that the tasks can be learned. Herrnstein and Loveland (1964) trained a pigeon to peck only when a picture containing a person was present; and in later experiments Herrnstein and his colleagues have demonstrated discrimination of one particular person, of triangles from other geometrical figures, trees from non-trees, oak leaves from other leaves, and so forth. The importance of these experiments is that the stimuli to be discriminated are defined in terms of broad, natural categories. There is no simple perceptual dimension, like size or colour, which the pigeon can use to distinguish people from non-people. According to philosophers such as Wittgenstein (1953/1968) or Ryle (1949), the absence of any simple defining feature is a characteristic property of human concepts; it is also one of the hardest to handle in any simple computer model of human intelligence.

Concepts discriminated in this way are sometimes described as higher-order stimulus classes, just because no simple perceptual dimensions will define them. With some animals, it is also possible to establish higher-order response classes. For example Hayes and Hayes (1952) taught a chimpanzee, Viki, an imitation set:

whenever Viki responded to the order 'Do this, Viki', by imitating the experimenter's actions, she was rewarded. Quite complex skills can be taught to chimpanzees in this way. Another higher-order response class was established in an experiment by Pryor, Haag and O'Reilly (1969) using a rough-toothed porpoise. The porpoise was kept in a dolphinarium where she performed acrobatics for an audience. Pryor and her colleagues decided to transfer the task of thinking up new acrobatic tricks to the porpoise. They established a regime where she was only rewarded with fish for a trick if it was one that she had never been rewarded for performing before. Of course, this cuts right across all normal principles of response-shaping, since the moment any response was rewarded it was no longer appropriate to repeat it. Only the higher-order response class of 'novelty' was consistently reinforced. Yet within sixteen twenty-minute sessions, the porpoise was consistently producing novel responses and being rewarded for them; by session thirty-two her behaviour had become so complex that the experimenters could no longer describe it.

Language in apes

Impressive though some of these demonstrations of animal intelligence are, the ultimate and best-known *tours de force* in this area are undoubtedly the various projects which have claimed to teach some form of language to various species of ape, mainly to chimpanzees. This section can only give the briefest summary of this fascinating and disputatious literature.

Many years ago, attempts were made to teach chimpanzees spoken language. Hayes and Hayes (1952) gave Viki, their young chimpanzee, intensive training in language use, relying heavily on the generalized imitation set mentioned earlier. Viki learned many skills in her brief life, but she only learned about four sounds, and none of them was very language-like in use (Hayes and Nissen, 1971). In a pre-war project (described by Kellogg, 1968) a more passive procedure was used. A young chimpanzee called Gua was brought up alongside the Kellogg's son Donald, and so far as possible the two were treated alike. Gua certainly came to treat the Kelloggs as his parents (for instance, he showed the usual juvenile chimpanzee tendency to interfere with his mother's copulation and as a result had to be excluded from the Kelloggs' bedroom), but he did not learn to speak, whereas Donald, of course, did.

It is now known that these projects were foredoomed, in that the chimpanzee's vocal tract is simply not adapted to produce human speech or anything like it. But actual speech seems to be a relatively superficial characteristic of language, and more recent projects have tried to teach apes forms of language that do not involve speech. Premack (1976) taught a chimpanzee called Sarah to use coloured plastic chips that could be attached to a magnetized board; Gardner and Gardner (1971) taught a chimpanzee called Washoe to use American sign language, a gestural form of communication used by deaf people; and Rumbaugh (1977) taught a chimpanzee called Lana to respond to symbols placed on a modified computer keyboard. All these projects were successful at least in their authors' eyes, and all have been followed up by their authors and others with additional animals (sometimes of other ape species), modified techniques and continued reported success. All, though, have been received with scepticism in many quarters, and there have been some replications which have led their authors to conclude that whatever the apes were learning it could not be called language. For example, Terrace (1979) applied the technique the Gardners had used with Washoe to a young chimpanzee called Nim, and concluded that the entire performance could be understood in terms of fairly simple conditioning procedures, which he is now trying to demonstrate in operation with pigeons.

What can we conclude? These experiments certainly succeeded in teaching apes something nearer to human language than anything they had been taught before. There is no doubt that in their different ways Sarah, Washoe, Lana and their successors have been able to signal for distinct objects (e.g. toys or kinds of food) and request distinct actions (e.g. being tickled or taken for a walk). It has been possible to use the 'language' systems to test chimpanzees' abstract logical capacities in new ways, as in a recent series of experiments on Sarah by Premack and his colleagues (Gillan, 1982), demonstrating for example that she is capable of analogical reasoning of the kind often included in intelligence tests for human children. Two things, though, are notably lacking. The first is much in the way of spontaneous comment from the apes. In the Gardners' film of Washoe, at only one point does she seem to be using a sign for anything beyond replying to a sign made to her or making a direct request. That is in a sequence where she escapes from a test situation and swings wildly about the enclosure making the sign for 'dirty'. The resemblance to a small child running away from a harassed parent, shouting 'knickers!' is irresistible; but it may be relevant to note that servicemen who lose the power to speak because of bullet wounds in the brain occasionally retain the power to swear freely. It may be that this kind of emotionally laden use of language is a different function from language proper. A few other spontaneous utterances have been recorded: the Gardners make much, for example, of Washoe putting her doll into her mug and then signing 'baby in my drink'. But the point about these records is that they are few. You do not have to spend much time with a 3-year-old child, with not much more than Washoe's alleged power of language, before you hear a whole stream of what is called 'egocentric speech' – spontaneous comment on what the child is doing. So far this has not been reported on nearly the same scale for any ape. Nor do apes seem to have much to say to strangers, even strangers fluent in whatever language the ape has been taught.

The other kind of evidence that is notably lacking from the 'ape language' experiments is much to suggest that the apes use their newly acquired languages to communicate with one another. It is only fair to say that attempts to encourage them to do this are as yet in their infancy, and in any case it may be that the apes have their own means of communicating anything they want to tell one another (or, remembering chapter 3, anything they may want to lie to one another about). But this opens the whole question of the passing of information from one organism to another, and this needs to be looked at in a broader framework.

Cultural transmission of behaviour

We know that animals can influence one another's behaviour in a variety of ways. The simple signalling instincts studied by the comparative ethologists are one example. Another is imitative learning, whether in relatively constrained contexts like the way a chaffinch learns its song from the previous generation, or in the broader sense in which a primate may be able to acquire an imitation set, and so come to imitate an arbitrary response so long as it is made with the right prior signals or by the right model.

We believe that the communicative capacities involved here are carried in the animal's genes, whether it is a matter of a simple Lorenzian IRM or a general learning capacity. But once one animal's behaviour can influence another's, we have the potential for another means, over and above genetic inheritance, by which behaviour can be perpetuated from generation to generation. And if anything is being passed on in this way, it can also be changed in the process. Processes like those of natural selection will begin to apply. The stage is set for what we can term 'cultural transmission' of behaviour, and its inevitable concomitant, 'cultural evolution'. The systematic study of these two processes is only just beginning, and it promises to be one of the most exciting areas in behavioural biology over the next few years. A simple introduction is given by Pulliam and Dunford (1980).

Let us consider some of the behaviour patterns which we already know to be culturally transmitted, at least in part. Chaffinch song is a good example: if each individual male chaffinch could not hear the song of its father's generation, then chaffinch song would revert to subsong within a generation. Another concerns the lekking grounds of the Uganda kob: these antelope use the same sites for their leks year after year, and within the lekking ground it is the same positions, year after year, which are most sought after. Yet there seems to be nothing objectively preferable about these areas; it is simply that the herd 'knows', by cultural transmission, that certain leks are the ones to fight for, because they were last year. A third is paternal care in the Japanese macaque (Itani, 1959). As was mentioned in chapter 5, in some troops of these monkeys adult males provide some degree of care for yearlings when the new infants are born. The interesting point is that, according to Itani, this behaviour originated in one male in just one of the eighteen troops that Japanese primatologists have under long-term study on the so-called 'Monkey Island'. This was the Minoo B troop, and paternal care rapidly spread through it. Now, however, this troop has grown to such an extent that it has split into two, and emigrating males have also taken paternal care to a third troop, where it has spread to the males who were there before the emigrants arrived. This looks very much like a process of cultural evolution at work.

There are other examples of cultural transmission of behaviour. Two of the most striking come from a single female in that same Minoo B troop of the Japanese macaques (Itani, 1958). The primatologists buried some sweet potatoes in the sandy beach of the island, to see whether the monkeys would find and eat them. In due course they did; but one female, at the time a juvenile, developed the habit of washing the potatoes in the sea to remove the sand. This behaviour eventually spread right across the island, by an interesting and consistent route: it was first taken up by other juveniles, next by adult females, last of all by adult males. The same female made another successful invention when the experimenters buried rice instead of potatoes: she learned to throw a mixture of sand and rice onto the water, then recover the rice, which floated (the sand, of course, did not). This behaviour, too, has since spread.

The evolution of human intelligence

What we have seen in this chapter should be enough to make us realize that no human behaviour could ever be wholly determined by genetic factors. Animals of all sorts have a great range of learning capacities, which to a greater or lesser extent modify their behaviour and add to the relatively restricted possibilites laid down by Lorenzian IRMs. Even cultural transmission from generation to generation and from group to group is well established in animal species. Everything we know about ourselves tells us that these factors will be much more powerful in humans than in other animals.

But why should our learning capacities be so much greater than those of other species? Does what we have discovered about learning in this chapter give us any hint of the conditions that might have caused its importance to increase dramatically? What ecological or other factors predispose animals to have advanced learning abilities?

The first question to ask is whether our learning capacities really are that extraordinary. Certainly our achievements are, but they are cumulative. It could be that we are only fractionally more intelligent than chimpanzees (whatever such a comparison might mean), but that the difference is just enough to allow us to pass on information from generation to generation in a way that other species cannot. Or it might be that our general learning abilities (as discovered in habituation, conditioning or even imitation learning, for example) are quite modest, but that we have one key special learning ability. Other species have these too, but the ability to learn to home does not lift a pigeon into a totally different class of organisms; the ability to learn to speak might lift a human being there. That, broadly, is the position I shall take up in the next chapter.

We still have to ask why we should have evolved this special ability. It is no answer to point to our large brains. Fossil evidence suggests that many crucial changes in the behaviour of prehominids and hominids had taken place before the 'big brain' evolved (Reynolds, 1980, chapter 5). The big brain could in fact be a consequence of our language or other special capacities rather than a cause of them; the development of special cognitive powers may have been what gave a selective advantage to individuals with larger brains. In any case, all primates have relatively large brains. Jerison (1973, chapter 2) has shown that, across all birds and mammals, there is a consistent relationship between brain weight and body weight, but that those species we think of as 'intelligent' – wolves, crows, porpoises and primates – have large brains for their body size. Human beings may simply have taken to extremes a tendency that already existed in the group from which we sprang.

Many hypotheses have been put forward to explain the evolution of language and intelligence in our species. In the light of what we have learned in this chapter and elsewhere in the book, two factors seem particularly plausible. The first is the fact that early hominids and prehominids were probably social hunters and gatherers. We saw earlier that foraging is a likely selective pressure on learning capacities; social hunting imposes special demands, of co-ordination between individuals, and most social hunters we know are of relatively high intelligence. Hunting should particularly favour the evolution of advanced means of communication.

The hunting hypothesis is widely accepted as at least part of the story. The second idea I should like to put forward is more contentious, but it has considerable appeal in terms of ideas developed elsewhere in this book. It was proposed by Alison Jolly (1966) and Nicholas Humphrey (1976). The Jolly–Humphrey thesis is that the advanced intelligence within the primate order, and humans' exceptional intelligence, developed through the demands of the complex networks of relationship, alliance and deceit that are a feature of any primate troop. Imagine an individual who was exceptionally good at keeping track of who his relatives were, of who could be exploited without risk, of who had done him a good turn which must be repaid if another was to be forthcoming, and also of how all the other individuals in the group were associated by such links of kinship, dominance and obligation. Such an individual would be in a powerful position to secure genetic advantages, and his genes would tend to spread. But as this happened, the level of intelligence required to secure an advantage would rise. The stage would be set for a positive feedback process, leading to an explosive expansion of intelligence. Of course, the potential for this process would exist in any primate species, and we have to ask why it took off only in the hominids. Perhaps the fact that they alone were hunters provided the crucial extra factor.

Regardless of how it came about, however, there is no room for doubt that human beings have at least some exceptional learning capacities. In the next and final chapter we consider how this modifies our approach to understanding the behaviour of our own species.

7

The talking animal

Human beings are unique among animals, for every species of animal is unique. Yet we feel that the gap between ourselves and the great apes is much wider than the gap between, say, a willow warbler and a chiff-chaff – two species so similar that a human bird-watcher can only distinguish them by song, and there is no evidence that either the willow warbler or the chiff-chaff has any other means of telling the difference.

Some of the differences between us and the apes are structural. Humans are the only kind of mammal that is convincingly bipedal, almost hairless and endowed with a brain whose mass is overwhelmingly concentrated into the cerebral cortex. But the differences we get excited about are behavioural. This chapter is about the behavioural uniqueness of the human species. What, precisely, is unique about us? What are the causes of our unique qualities? How do they affect the use we can make of other animals' behaviour in interpreting our own? These are the questions we shall be trying to answer.

For me, they are the questions that give the study of ethology its spice and zest. Some scientists pour time, effort and money into trying to make contact with other intelligences on other planets. I have no difficulty in understanding that. They are spurred by a fundamental question about human existence: are we alone in the universe? The same question drives me to look at the other animal species that share our own small green planet. Are we humans, in all the important ways, alone on the Earth? Or are there other intelligences here, too, with whom we could make better contact than we now do?

What kind of special case is the human species?

Granted that every species is unique, what are the features that define the human species? We glanced at some of our obvious structural oddities just now. There are other features of our bodies that may have behavioural implications. Our hand structure is different from that of a typical ape such as a gibbon, which has much longer fingers and much less versatile thumbs. We can make very little use of our feet and toes for grasping objects, presumably because of adaptations to our two-legged way of getting about. That has another consequence, too: it forces changes in pelvic structure which, together with our large heads, mean that our babies have to be born in a much less developed state than typical newborn apes. And, quite simply, we are rather large, though for our size neither very heavy nor very strong.

Other branches of biology, besides anatomy, have something to say about human uniqueness. From genetics we learn that the DNA in our chromosomes is for 99 per cent of its length identical to that of a chimpanzee. From ecology we learn that the human species is uniquely adaptable. More than any other species, we are found across almost the complete range of continents, temperatures, vegetation types, altitudes, or any other ecological parameter you care to think of. The only ecological barrier we do not cross is that between land and water: if we except nuclear submariners, there are no humans who are truly at home in rivers, lakes or sea.

But why should we except nuclear submariners? They, and more especially the 'aquanauts' who inhabit experimental stations like the Americans' Sealab, have the capability to live under the sea. We feel that this is not a fair example because it is only possible because of advanced human technology. But it is only technology that enables an Eskimo to survive in Greenland or the Canadian Arctic. Which is bigger – the step from the sealskin coat and igloo to the nuclear submarine, or from the chimpanzee's nest of twigs to the igloo and coat? The time the two steps have taken suggests that the crucial step is the one that gave us 'primitive' technology. From there to the nuclear submarine – and the nuclear bomb – is a straightforward, seemingly inevitable and rapidly accelerating progression.

Technology is a kind of behaviour. Is it the crucial kind? A popular view holds that it is: *Homo faber*, man the maker, man the tool-user, is a key alias for *Homo sapiens*. But there are plenty of rival views. We have looked at the idea that man (it seems right to use the male form here) is the uniquely aggressive animal. Others point to our great cities, our organized states and empires, and talk about human beings as 'the social animal' – the title of Aronson's (1972) well-known introductory text on social psychology. Equally valid would be to point to the very long period in which young humans are dependent on their parents. Although this period varies from culture to culture, and although apes too can have lengthy dependent periods (remember the 8-year-old chimpanzee Flint, who starved and died after the death of his mother, Flo), it would be perfectly plausible to refer to us as 'the parenting animal'.

My view in this book is an older one, though still the dominant one. I hold that the kind of behaviour that makes the difference between us and the apes is, above all, language. Hence the title of this chapter: 'The talking animal'. In one form or another, this view has dominated philosophy, at least in the west, for as long as people have thought about the kinds of question raised at the beginning of this chapter. It lies behind the traditional Christian doctrine that humans have immortal souls but animals do not: what we call our soul or mind is the part of ourselves with which we can have an internal dialogue (to beg a few questions in theology and ego psychology, but never mind). For Aristotle, though other animals might have souls, to speak was to be human. And it has been repeated *ad nauseam* in the past decade or two by psychologists arguing that nothing an animal does, whether in the field under the eyes of an ethologist or in the laboratory under the eyes of an operant behaviourist, can be of any possible relevance to understanding human cognition and human behaviour.

Language seems to be the key to our progressive cultural development, and to the way cultural determination takes over from genetic determination when we care to consider human behaviour.

None the less, there are objections to the view that the key to human uniqueness is language behaviour. There are other philosophical traditions besides the western. Hinduism and Buddhism, and many local animistic religions, see all animals (even in some cases plants and inanimate objects) as having souls, and this opinion existed even in Greek philosophy, most famously in the teachings of Pythagoras. Europeans are as ready as anyone to attribute powers of linguistic communication to other animals. We talk to our pets and farm animals, we imagine that they talk to each other, and we believe all too readily any psychologist or ethologist who tells us that he or she has taught sign language to a gorilla, found a subtle system of chemical signals among hunting dogs or intercepted advanced communications between dolphins. Thus the lay person's perceptions do not always take language as uniquely human. Scientific speculation, too, sometimes sees language as secondary to other aspects of human uniqueness. The brain structures essential to language are concentrated in one of the two cerebral hemispheres, usually the left, which also controls the normally dominant right hand. Could language be in some way a consequence of a pre-existing asymmetry of the human brain, evolved perhaps under the elective pressure of tool use (or weapon-making), in which the stronger left hand holds the work while the right hand does the skilled work of wielding the tool?

There are no answers yet to questions like these. We do not know when our prehominid and hominid ancestors became able to speak. We cannot yet trace the evolution of language in any useful detail. What we can do is to look at its consequences, both in making human behaviour different from animal behaviour and in changing the use we can make of evolution in understanding human behaviour.

The differences language makes

Although the influence of language on our behaviour is all-pervading, I want to focus on three particular points. They concern the way behaviour is controlled by our past, our present and our future. It is convenient to consider the future first.

In chapter 6 I argued that the need to forage optimally was a selective pressure of sufficient generality to account for the evolution of conditioning and its laws. But a human trying to get the maximum amount of prey in the minimum time is not at the mercy of the laws of conditioning, or whatever other foraging mechanism evolution may have endowed us with. If I am planning a blackberrying expedition, I can sit down and work out in advance what the optimal foraging strategy will be, and use my calculations to draw up rules which will enable me to forage optimally. In a word, I can approach the problem *rationally*: we humans are capable of rational foresight. Economists (and psychologists, for whom there is less excuse) often use the word 'rational' as a synonym for 'optimal', but this is to mistake function for mechanism. Humans and other animals can both achieve optimal behaviour in certain environments but, so far as we know, only humans can do it by previewing in imagination the consequences of different courses of behaviour. Language may not always be necessary for this process, but in practice it nearly always seems to be involved. Oddly enough it is the radical behaviourist Skinner (1969, chapter 6) who has written most clearly about this. He distinguishes *rule-governed* (i.e. rational) behaviour from *contingency-governed* behaviour (i.e. the kind of behaviour that can be understood in terms of conditioning principles). Rule-governed behaviour, Skinner argues, comes to the fore in human problem-solving. Of course, to reason about a problem is not always to arrive at an optimal solution, and in some cases it may be best to leave matters to the principles of conditioning or to our instincts. But language clearly gives us a powerful new way in which our behaviour can be influenced by its own future consequences, or by the future consequences of other events we perceive in our environment.

But talking and reasoning to ourselves sounds like a secondary use of language compared with communicating with others. The obvious difference language makes to behaviour lies in the present, in the way individuals in a human society can be influenced by other individuals. From an evolutionary standpoint, whether we think about the selective advantage conferred by good communication within a social hunting group, or of the selective advantage of good communication within a political clique, real language would bring added benefits, over and above simply increasing the amount of information that could be conveyed. When we looked at the literature on animals' concept-learning in chapter 6, we found some evidence that animals other than man can form and manipulate abstract concepts, but there is no doubt that the ability to give an abstraction a linguistic label, a name in other words, makes it very much easier to manipulate it. It has often been claimed that those congenitally deaf people who do not acquire a wide active vocabulary find it very difficult to understand abstractions (though this result is controversial). Would it be possible to have a concept of 'the day before yesterday' without language? Geach (1957) has doubted it. The same might be said for 'a second cousin on the mother's side, once removed', yet in the algebra of kin altruism there would be substantial advantage in being able to manipulate such concepts. Lévi-Strauss (1966) argues that much or all primitive symbolism and myth is to be understood as a metaphor for kinship concepts. Language clearly makes it easier for other individuals present in our society to be taken into account in the determination of our own behaviour, whether that behaviour involves co-operative hunting or internecine conspiracy.

Of all the ways in which language affects us, though, the most overwhelming is surely the way it allows the past to influence our present behaviour. It is language that makes possible the cumulative culture of human beings. We have seen that animals too have culture of a sort. But humans can tell each other what happened a generation, a century or a millennium ago.

Newton remarked that, if he had seen further, it was because he had stood on the shoulders of giants. But a human being does not have to be either Newton or an intellectual giant to see infinitely further than any chimpanzee. Each one of us stands on the shoulders of thousands of generations of previous humans, and it is language that ensures that the innumerable tiny insights and innovations of each generation are built together into the pyramid of knowledge and technology which gives us our favoured standpoint. Given language, an individual human need not be more than a tiny fraction more intelligent than another animal to seem to belong to a totally different order of intellectual ability.

Cultural evolution and genetic evolution

Through language, we benefit from the experience and wisdom of all previous generations of people: that is what we mean by 'culture'. Surely, though, it is far too formidable a task for each new human to learn the history of all former humans? But of course that is not what happens. Human experience selects certain information as worth passing on to a new generation. It is easy to think of this process as conscious and deliberate: we think in terms of governments (or, in Britain, the teaching profession) deciding what material to include in the school curriculum. This is the least important aspect of culture. What matters are the rules of behaviour – manners, morals, strategy – we pick up from our elders, usually by unconscious imitation rather than conscious imitation or deliberate instruction; and, pervading everything else, our language itself. All these things undergo slow processes of change over generations. Mostly, these changes are not a result of anyone's policy; they 'just happen'.

One of the most compelling insights of recent years is that behavioural biologists cannot be content to think of changes in culture 'just happening', any more than we can consider the changes from one species to another as 'just happening'. A process like natural selection must be at work. The idea that such a process exists has come to be known as the theory of 'cultural evolution'.

Dawkins (1976) coined the word 'meme' to describe the unit of information that would be susceptible to selection by cultural means. I prefer the more familiar word 'idea'. The basis of the modern theory of cultural evolution is to take the analogy between genes and ideas seriously, and see where it leads us. Of course, genes and ideas do not have the same conceptual status. The physical basis of genes is known, that of ideas is not. Individuals can do nothing about the genes they contain, but they can at least influence what ideas they acquire. But both genes and ideas are contained within individuals, influence those individuals' behaviour, yet can survive after the individual's death. There is enough commonality here to make the analogy interesting.

What determines whether an idea will survive within the pool of ideas that constitutes a culture? Dawkins argues that the requirements are the same as those for the survival of genes within a gene pool. A successful gene must be long-lived, must tend to replicate itself precisely, must be highly fecund (i.e. it must replicate rapidly and frequently) and, finally, must be ruthlessly selfish in direct competition with other replicators. In the case of genes, the relevant competition is not between individual organisms, though, it is between alleles – different genes that can occupy the same locus (position on the DNA that constitutes the chromosome of a single organism). In the case of ideas, presumably the corresponding competition is between ideas about the same subject matter. The idea that the moon is made of green cheese competes with the idea that it is a lump of sterile rock. The idea that it is acceptable to abort an unwanted foetus competes with the idea that abortion is morally wrong.

Genes that are not alleles of each other sometimes come into conflict. The striated finch is a distance species, and it has a tendency, which we believe to be genetically determined, to keep a set minimum distance from its conspecifics. It also has a tendency, which we also believe to be genetically determined, to copulate with its conspecifics under appropriate circumstances. The genes for both these tendencies have been successful. They are not alleles of each other. Yet when they find simultaneous expression, they are incompatible, and the result is the approach–avoid conflict we examined in chapter 3. Similarly, ideas that are not in direct competition may be incompatible, and this may lead to conflict when they find simultaneous expression. The idea that it is wrong to kill other human beings is incompatible with the idea that it is right to do anything to defend one's native country, but they are not concerned with the same immediate subject. It is only if both ideas find simultaneous expression that the individual possessing them is thrown into conflict. If one gene and another, both successful at their locus, and one idea and another, both also successful in their context, may come into conflict, might not a gene and an idea also come into conflict? Clearly they might, and it is not obvious in advance which would win.

But of course our chief reason for being interested in either genes or ideas is the way in which, by their own imperatives for survival, they affect the behaviour of the individuals that carry them. On the whole, the requirement that genes should be fecund and long-lived means that they tend to produce individuals who are fecund and long-lived. But we have seen how gene selfishness need not imply individual selfishness, at least as regards kin. This can be put another way: the interests of an organism's genes are not always the same as the organism's interests, if we take the organism to be interested in a long and pleasurable life. It is just the same with ideas. On the whole, they will be successful if they tend to make the individuals that carry them successful. But an idea that ensured that, if one individual laid down his life, two others who shared his idea would survive, would be selected in the cultural pool just as surely as a gene for sacrificing yourself in favour of four full siblings would be selected in the gene pool. We have also seen that the interests of the genes are not always the interests of the group, population or species that carries them. Again it is the same with ideas. The idea of tax avoidance is socially disruptive; it is none the less very hard to eradicate from the pool of ideas in our society.

Finally, we come back to the interactions between genetic and cultural selection. Where a behaviour is adaptive, it could be produced by either genetic or cultural evolution, and it will never be easy to disentangle which is responsible. Occasionally, however, we may find the two in conflict. Genetic selection tells us to lay down our own lives to save the lives of (enough of) those who share our genes. Cultural selection tells us to lay down our lives to save the lives of (enough of) those who share our ideas. The two groups will not always coincide: what if my brothers are in deadly conflict with my coreligionists? On whose behalf should I intervene? Common speech says that genetic selection is the more powerful pressure: 'Blood is thicker than water' is a common phrase, while it took Jesus of Nazareth to say of a crowd of his disciples, 'Here are my mother and my brothers.' But the issue cannot be regarded as closed. The so-called 'sociobiology debate' (Caplan, 1978) involved heated denunciations of Wilson and other sociobiologists, just on the grounds that they are proposing a biological determinism – arguing that human behaviour can be understood in terms of genetic-selection pressures rather than culture. It is time for us to see whether human behaviour can be biologically determined.

Are human instincts evolutionarily conservative?

We know that humans have at least some instincts, in the full Lorenzian sense. We know too that we have instincts in the broader sense of general motivational tendencies such as hunger, thirst, sexuality or parental concern, though these are much harder to describe and document objectively. No one doubts that these instincts are of genetic origin. Should we see their existence as evidence for a more general biological determination of human behaviour? Or should we see them as exceptions, which test the rule that human behaviour is normally determined by culture, and by their exceptional character establish its accuracy?

What kind of exception could these human instincts be? There seem to be only two possibilities. One is that they concern behaviours on which the genetic selective pressures are strong, while the cultural selective pressures are weak. The other is that instincts involve behaviours that are 'evolutionarily conservative', that is they are unusually resistant to change under any selective force.

Probably some human instincts have survived because, for the behaviour they determine, cultural selection is weak relative to genetic selection. Several of the clearest and most Lorenzian instincts are behaviours of very young babies or behaviours towards very young babies. The cultural pressures on a newborn baby are obviously weak: even a practice like swaddling seems likely to submerge instinctive infant behaviour rather than modify it. And since behaviours towards young babies are partly controlled by the responses the babies make in return, this weakness of cultural control will extend to parents to some extent (not completely, as the rapid changes in child-care fashions remind us).

Equally, it is easy to see that instincts in the broader motivational sense should be under strong genetic pressure. There are likely to be severe genetic consequences for humans who feel no hunger or feel no interest in the opposite sex. But it is also easy to see why such broad tendencies should be evolutionarily conservative. The general pattern of life seems to be that evolution modifies means much faster than it modifies ends. The secondary structure of insulin is slightly different in different mammals; the function it performs is not. Teeth vary so much that they are one of the morphologist's best ways of differentiating species, but in every species their chief function is to process food. Different species of ducks have different-coloured specula on their wings, but all use them in courtship displays.

The disputed ground comes somewhere between the small-scale action and the broad motivational tendency. Everyone would grant that for a person to go out, find food and bring it back to share with his or her family involves several instinctive tendencies. Everyone would equally grant that the means by which that person obtains food – the bow and arrows, fishing spear or gardening tools – is a product of culture. But what about the intermediate level? What about the fact that it is usually the man rather than the woman in a family who goes out to hunt? What about the way the food is shared between the individuals in the group? What about the fact that some foods are acceptable whereas others are not? How do genetic and cultural evolution interact at this level? Broad arguments about the strength of selection pressures cannot help us here.

Do we fit into a biological pattern?

One alternative approach is to ask whether our species fits into a pattern that we can see running across a range of related species. Do humans show tendencies that are typical of other primates? Do human societies show tendencies that are typical of other primate societies? There will be differences, of course, for every species is different, but do we fit into the general scheme of things or stand out from it as breaking all the rules?

Consider first something which is not in itself a behavioural trait but is widely believed to have an influence on behaviour: brain size. On the one hand, the human brain is a typical primate brain: relative to the average mammalian brain, it is large for our body size and its mass is concentrated in the forebrain and especially the cerebral cortex. Furthermore, these trends are seen more and more strongly as we move from prosimians, the primates believed to be least closely related to man, through the increasingly closely related monkeys, lesser apes and great apes (though in some respects human brain organization resembles that of the New World spider monkey more than that of the chimpanzee). On the other hand, no other primate takes this trend to anything like the extreme our species achieves. We seem to be both typical and exceptional.

Brain size is commonly supposed to determine learning capacity. Is human learning typical of primate learning? Evidently in one vital respect it is not, for as we have seen other primates have at best learnt only the beginnings of language. All other forms of learning are likely to be mediated by language to some extent. If we do what psychologists have been striving to do for over a century, and set up learning situations where the influence of language is minimized, we find a story similar to that for brain size. If we use 'arbitrary' stimuli and responses, of no particular biological significance, primates show better learning than other species, and the closer they are to humans, the better they tend to learn; humans learn better than any. But across non-human species these trends are weak enough to have been disputed by some (Macphail, 1982, for example), and when we try to include humans in our analysis, we find that it is very difficult to be sure that we have excluded the human verbal reasoning mode from any problem-solving situation.

Consider now a behaviour which, in other animals at least, we are prepared to call instinctive, the care of the young. We have seen that there are some Lorenzian instincts involved in human mother–child interactions. But can we go further than that? Is there a general 'mothering instinct'? Is the long period of human dependency a typical primate pattern? Once again we find that humans are both typical and exceptional members of the primate order. Almost all primates take several years to reach maturity, rather than the one which is common in other mammals. The period of immaturity is typically spent in association with the parents, and with some degree of dependence on them, and is associated with an extended birth interval at least in the great apes. Yet the human dependent period is the longest of all, and it is also influenced by culture in very obvious ways. In the degenerate Ik society studied by Colin Turnbull (1973), children were turned out to fend for themselves at the age of 3 or 4; in the middle-class England of the Victorian era, children could be not just dependent on their parents, but largely subject to them, until the age of 21 or even older.

The example of child care raises one of the most sensitive questions in the whole area of the interaction of biology and culture, that of the roles and relations of the sexes. Is human society typical of primate societies in the roles it allocates to male and female, for example in hunting being most often a male activity while child-rearing tends to be a female responsibility? Part of the difficulty of answering this question is that it is not at all clear what is typical of human society. What society should we be comparing with the societies of our fellow primates? The society of the !Kung bushmen and other hunter-gatherers, who are thought to live in much the same way as our pre-hominid ancestors? The society of the prosperous western nations of the twentieth century? Or perhaps the society of an Israeli kibbutz, or of the promiscuous Polynesians reported by Margaret Mead (1943), or of the polyandrous Tibetans studied by Goldstein (1971)? As I pointed out in chapter 5, nearly all our words for describing animal societies are borrowed from anthropology. Almost every conceivable kind of society is found in some human group somewhere, and this is true most especially of mating systems, which obviously have an enormous influence on sex roles. In the face of this variation, can we even sensibly ask whether human society is typical of primate societies?

We can, because there are consistencies and trends that run through the great variety of human societies. Burton, Brudner and White (1977) give several examples concerned with division of labour in a sample of 185 different societies. Take the various jobs involved in processing animal products, from butchering the animal to preserving meat and manufacturing clothing. All are performed by men in some cultures and women in others. But the pattern of sex roles is not random. While there are many societies in which men butcher animals and women manufacture clothing, there are none in the sample where the reverse holds: in fact there is a chain of sub-tasks such that if women perform one sub-task, they will certainly perform all sub-tasks further along the chain. Similar 'implication chains' exist for animal care, fishing and vegetable food processing. In every case, the sub-tasks on the male end of the chain are those that have to be performed less often and are more complex in themselves. As Douglas and Isherwood (1979) have explained, such 'low frequency tasks' tend to be associated with greater pleasure, prestige and power. Male dominance over women appears to be a common property of human societies.

Mating systems can be considered in a similar way. Although almost every kind of mating system we encounter in animal societies has its counterpart in some human culture, the distribution is by no means random. Unless our data base is hopelessly distorted by sexist biases among anthropologists, polygyny is much more common than polyandry, an interesting reflection of the general situation among vertebrates. Furthermore, the incidence of mating systems is related to ecology within the human species in the same way as it is between species in the rest of the animal kingdom. If there are any truly promiscuous human societies (which has been questioned: Symons, 1979), they occur where resources are abundant, as in Polynesia; polygyny, especially in its extreme forms, is also associated with natural wealth. The colder, ecologically (or economically) more difficult conditions of northern Europe have called forth instead a tendency to pair-bonding. Polyandry is confined to desperately harsh environments such as Tibet, the Arctic or rural Iceland, and there, as in other animal species, the several husbands of one wife are most often brothers or other close relatives.

How do cultural and genetic selection pressures contribute to this pattern? There is no reason to suppose that, because genetic differences between chickens and turkeys ensure that chickens are polygynous while turkeys are polyandrous, it is genetic differences between Tibetans and Samoans that produce their different mating systems.

Ecological constraints will select as inexorably between ideas, in a species capable of holding them, as they select between genes in all species. It is interesting to note that pair-bonding in northern European and North American human societies, and the moral and cultural norms that have supported it, at present seem to be giving way to serial polygamy or promiscuity, both of which tend to leave one parent (usually the mother) supporting children on her own. It is hard to avoid the speculation that this is a result of technology mitigating ecological constraints. The ecology of the temperate zone remains harsh, but its economy is buoyant.

Does this drift away from pair-bonding imply that promiscuity or polygyny would be a more 'natural' form of human society? Certainly, as we have seen, it seems to be a typical one across human societies. In this respect at least, humans are typical primates. Furthermore, we fit into a pattern that holds across the primate species in general (and, indeed, more widely). As we saw in our discussion of animal societies, increasing polygamy tends to be associated with increasing difference in size and appearance between male and female, the larger sex being the one that has many mates. Humans are moderately sexually dimorphic: our male/female weight ratio (about 1.25:1) is higher than that of the faithfully pair-bonding marmoset, but lower than that of the promiscuous chimpanzee or the invariably polygynous gorilla (Clutton-Brock and Harvey, 1977). On this basis, we should expect humans to be moderately polygynous, and over the range of our habitats that seems to be the average condition. So far as I know, however, human sexual dimorphism does not vary with ecological conditions, which strongly suggests that any correlation between ecology and human mating systems is maintained by cultural rather than genetic selection.

The conclusions from this section will doubtless satisfy no one. There are no clear-cut answers on offer. Human beings are both typical primates and extraordinary ones. Human societies both fit into the pattern of primate (and vertebrate) societies and transcend it. Some aspects of human behaviour and human society accord with what we should expect from general considerations of comparative and social ethology, but it is impossible to say whether that is a result of genetic selection, or cultural selection, or some interaction between them.

The abuse of animal behaviour

It is against this uncertain background that we have to decide the relevance of ethology to human behaviour. Clearly our decision is going to be provisional for a long time yet, until the contributions of genetic and cultural selection have been substantially clarified, and until the extent to which they follow similar laws has been sorted out. But some limited conclusions can be drawn, both positive and negative. This section deals with the negative aspect, asking what kinds of application of ethology are clearly unjustified. Three examples will be considered.

One of the most obvious can be dubbed the 'any animal will do' approach. Because sexually sated bulls show renewed potency when offered a new partner, it is held that sexual variety must be stimulating to humans. Because sticklebacks can be rewarded by the opportunity to fight, it is held that humans must be innate seekers of aggression. Because rhesus monkeys reared in isolation are socially incompetent as adults, it is held that children of 'broken homes' are liable to be delinquent. Anyone who has read a little popular ethology or, alas, academic psychology is likely to have encountered arguments of this sort. It should by now be obvious why they are invalid. Instincts and social structures are both adaptations to particular physical and social environments. Even if humans can be seen to be under the same selection pressures as cattle, sticklebacks or rhesus, we do not start from the same genetic constitution, and there can be no guarantee that we are following the same evolutionary pathway. Analogies between human and animal behaviour can only be useful if they are based on broad tendencies applying across the whole animal kingdom and supported by ecological and phylogenetic arguments showing how those tendencies are likely to be expressed in the human species. Comparative psychologists, with their notoriously excessive reliance on a few inbred strains of a few species, need to take special note of this.

A second way of abusing ethology involves what I call the 'self-terminating search', where you start with a particular kind of human behaviour in mind and seek a warrant for its naturalness by hunting for animal species that show comparable behaviour. In the animal kingdom, as in the Bible, you can find anything you are looking for, if you look for long enough and stop looking when you have found it. You can find large numbers of species that show female dominance over males, or male dominance over females; co-operative sharing or ruthless competition; parental care or parental neglect; or whatever else about human behaviour interests you. Some of the most serious writers on ethology and sociobiology could be accused of this error (reviewers usually call it 'selecting examples', but that is to impute malice). The cure is the same as in the previous case: in applying ethology we have to make rigorous attempts to ensure that the behaviours we cite are representative of the generality of animal species, and that we understand the phylogenetic and ecological context of the species that display them.

Finally, it simply will not do to ignore the influence of culture on human behaviour. Language is not just a more advanced form of the kinds of communication all vertebrates show. It makes it possible for the future, the present but above all the past to determine our behaviour in ways that scarcely apply at all to the rest of the animal kingdom, so far as we understand it at present. Cultures, like chromosomes, are products of selective pressures, and we do not expect that cultural and genetic selection will often be in conflict over essentials – but this means only that it will never be easy to say which is determining human behaviour. Apparent conflicts often dissolve on closer examination. Consider for example the love and effort expended on adoptive children. Because different societies have different norms for when and how children are adopted, while there is never any apparent genetic advantage in adoption at all, Sahlins (1977) has pointed to adoption as a case where cultural norms take precedence over genetic selection pressures. But if we consider how the genetic imperative to care for your own children could be implemented in terms of proximal mechanisms, it is clear that it would be genetically advantageous to form an affectional bond with any very young child who was put into your care, and to feel a need to care for such children. Conversely, consider the typical (though not universal) male dominance over women, accompanied by moderate polygyny. This looks at first sight like a typical primate pattern, resulting from typical sociobiological pressures – until we find that the variation in the extent of its expression between human societies is almost certainly without any genetic basis: children adopted from one society into another seem to follow sexual mores of their adoptive society quite as well as its genetic children.

The use of ethology

Though the study of animal behaviour can be abused, that does not mean it has no proper use. As we saw in the first chapter of this book, there are ways of applying ethology (for example, in matters of animal husbandry or in methods of observing behaviour) which are not in dispute. But in my opinion there are also proper uses for ethology in the disputed area, where we try to apply its ideas and results to human behaviour. In this final section I want to give a few examples which are, I feel, adequately supported by what I have said in the rest of the book.

First, by studying animal behaviour we are able to see what instincts are like when they are not confounded by culturally determined behaviours. This makes it much more likely that we will be able to recognize a human instinct on those (relatively rare) occasions when we meet one; it also gives us a much better chance of rejecting attempts (all too common) to label as 'instinctive' human behaviours or motivations which are nothing of the sort. As

Mary Midgley (1979) puts it, ethology tells us that there is such a thing as human nature, and it tells us at least something about what human nature is like, because ethology provides us with the tools to recognize and study instinctive behaviours.

Secondly, ethologists have discovered characteristics of instinctive behaviour which have obvious applications in human behaviour, but for one reason or another had not struck psychologists concentrating on the human case. To take three very obvious examples, the ideas of the dominance hierarchy, of individual distance and of displacement responding all have their origins in ethology. Of course the corresponding human phenomena had not gone unnoticed; it is scarcely news that human societies are sometimes hierarchical, or that people who do not know what to do fiddle with their clothes, or that you can make someone uncomfortable by standing too close to him or her. But ethology provided a framework within which those phenomena could be studied systematically and scientifically. It also offers one possible explanation for them, though for reasons stated above we always have to consider explanations coming from ethology alongside others of very different origins.

Finally, the study of animal behaviour does throw light on what makes us, as humans, different from other animals. If to be human is, above all, to be a talking animal, we need to understand what it is that language contributes to our life, and to understand that we have to know what life is like for animals without language. Much of what we think of as uniquely human can in fact be found elsewhere in the animal kingdom. Even our vaunted superior 'intelligence' is hard to demonstrate in a truly neutral context, where we are not employing language to aid us.

Comparative and social ethologists have mapped out a fair picture of the nature of animal behaviour and the selective pressures that have produced it, and this book has tried to sketch some of the main features of that picture. Do you recognize yourself in it? When you do something 'instinctively', is the way you respond really a fixed action pattern? When you quarrel with spouse or children, are you acting out the inevitable conflicts between sexes and generations predicted by the sociobiologists? Are the selective pressures that produced the language you speak, by cultural evolution, parallel to those that produced the vocal tract you speak with, by genetic evolution? I cannot yet answer these questions for you; in the present state of our knowledge they are still matters of opinion. If this book has made it possible for you to form your own opinions on them, it will have served its purpose.

Suggestions for further reading

General

Manning, A. (1979) *An Introduction to Animal Behaviour*, 3rd edn, London, Edward Arnold. This covers many of the same topics as the present book in greater detail, though with less emphasis on sociobiology and behavioural ecology.

Eibl-Eibesfeldt, I. (1975) *Ethology*, 2nd edn, New York, Holt, Rinehart & Winston. The best textbook of comparative ethology.

Dawkins, R. (1976) *The Selfish Gene*, London, Oxford University Press. The essential introduction to sociobiology – lively, provocative, aggressively Oxford.

Hinde, R.A. (1970) *Animal Behaviour*, 2nd edn, New York, McGraw-Hill; and Wilson, E.O. (1975) *Sociobiology*, Cambridge, Massachusetts, Harvard University Press. The reference texts – compendious, advanced, but not unreadable.

Chapter 1

Sheppard, P.M. (1975) *Natural Selection and Heredity*, 4th edn, London, Hutchinson. A good introduction to evolutionary theory for those with little or no biological background.

Gould, S.J. and Lewontin, R.C. (1979) 'The spandrels of San Marco and the Panglossian paradigm: a critique of the adaptionist programme', *Proceedings of the Royal Society*, Series B 205, 581–98. A pungent critique of 'adaptationism'.

Barash, D.P. (1982) *Sociobiology and Behaviour*, 2nd edn, London, Hodder & Stoughton. Chapters 2 and 3 give a more detailed account of genetics and evolution as they are applied in sociobiology.

Chapter 2

Tinbergen, N. (1951) *The Study of Instinct*, Oxford, Clarendon Press. Especially chapters 2 and 3. Still one of the freshest and best accounts of instinctive behaviour.

Hailman, J.P. (1969) 'How an instinct is learned', *Scientific American*, 221 (6), 98–106. A less 'classical' view of fixed action patterns than the one presented here.

Eibl-Eibesfeldt, I. (1975) op cit., Chapter 18, and (1979) 'Human ethology: concepts and implications for the science of man', *The Behavioral and Brain Sciences*, 2, 1–57, review work on human instincts.

Chapter 3

Lorenz, K.Z. (1958) 'The evolution of behaviour', *Scientific American*, 199 (6), 67–78. Exceptionally clear and, of course, authoritative on the classic ethological approach.

Bastock, M. (1967) *Courtship*, London, Heinemann. Chapters 4–7 give a detailed account of the evolution of courtship instincts.

Dawkins, R. and Krebs, J.R. (1978) 'Animal signals: information or manipulation?', in Krebs, J.R. and Davies, N.B. (eds) *Behavioural Ecology*, Oxford, Blackwell. A clear statement of the sociobiological view of signalling instincts.

Argyle, M. (1975) *Bodily Communication*, London, Methuen. An excellent overview of human paralanguage.

Chapter 4

Dawkins, (1976) op. cit. Especially chapters 5 and 6.

Barash (1982) op. cit. Chapters 5, 6, 9, 15 and 16.

Wilson, E.O. (1978) *On Human Nature*, Cambridge, Massachusetts, Harvard University Press. Chapters 5 and 7 for the human case.

Bertram, B.C.R. (1976) 'Kin selection in lions and evolution', in Bateson, P.P.G. and Hinde, R.A. (eds) *Growing Points in Ethology*, Cambridge, Cambridge University Press, 281–301. Gives an example of the kind of analysis proposed in this chapter.

Chapter 5

Barash (1982) op. cit. Chapters 10–14 for a more detailed sociobiological account of sex and parent roles.

Symons, D. (1979) *The Evolution of Human Sexuality*, New York, Oxford University Press. Especially chapters 5, 6 and 7 for the human case.

Hinde, R.A. and Spencer-Booth, Y. (1971) 'Effects of brief separation from mother on rhesus monkeys', *Science*, 173, 111–18. Gives a brief sane account of maternal deprivation in monkeys.

Short, R.V. (1979) 'Sexual selection and its component parts, somatic and genital selection, as illustrated by man and great apes', in Rosenblatt, J.S., Hinde, R.A., Beer, C. and Busnel, M-C. (eds) *Advances in the Study of Behavior*, vol. 9, New York, Academic Press, 131–58. An example of the kind of analysis discussed in this chapter.

Chapter 6

Tarpy, R.M. (1982) *Principles of Animal Learning and Motivation*, Glenview, Illinois, Scott Foresman. Chapters 2 and 6 give the necessary background in learning theory; or see Walker, S. (1984) *Learning Theory and Behaviour Modification*, London, Methuen.

Ristau, C.A. and Robbins, D. (1982) 'Cognitive aspects of ape language experiments', in Griffin, D.R. (ed.) *Animal Mind – Human Mind*, Berlin, Springer Verlag, 299–30. One of the many summaries of the ape language literature.

Bonner, J.T. (1980) *The Evolution of Culture in Animals*, Princeton, New Jersey, Princeton University Press. Summarizes the evidence for 'animal culture'.

Johnston, T.D. (1981) 'Contrasting approaches to a theory of learning', *Behavioral and Brain Sciences*, 4, 125–73. Another approach to the biology of learning.

Chapter 7

Wilson (1978) op. cit. A detailed and not too specialized treatment of sociobiology as applied to humans.

Pulliam, H.R. and Dunford, C. (1980) *Programmed to Learn*, New York, Columbia University Press. The best introduction to the topic of cultural evolution.

Midgley, M. (1979) *Beast and Man*, Brighton, Harvester (also available as a University Paperback from Methuen, London). This discusses at length the implications of ethology for our understanding of human beings.

References and name index

The numbers in italics following each entry refer to page numbers in this book.

Ardrey, R. (1961) *African Genesis*, New York, Dell. *60*

Argyle, M. (1975) *Bodily Communication*, London, Methuen. *46*

Aronson, E. (1972) *The Social Animal*, San Francisco, Freeman. *110*

Barnett, S.A. (1958) 'An analysis of social behaviour in wild rats', *Proceedings of the Zoological Society of London*, 130, 107–52. *56*

Bertram, B.C.R. (1976) 'Kin selection in lions and evolution', in Bateson, P.P.G. and Hinde, R.A. (eds) *Growing Points in Ethology*, Cambridge, Cambridge University Press, 281–301. *65*

Bertram, B.C.R. (1978) *Pride of Lions*, London, Dent. *50, 58*

Buechner, H.K. and Roth, H.D. (1974) 'The lek system in Uganda kob antelope', *American Zoologist*, 14, 145–62. *72*

Burton, M.L., Brudner, L.A. and White, D.R. (1977) 'A model of the sexual division of labor', *American Ethnologist*, 4, 227–51. *120*

Caplan, A.C. (1978) *The Sociobiology Debate*, New York, Harper & Row. *116*

Chitty, D. (1954) *Control of Rats and Mice*, vol. 1, Oxford, Clarendon Press. *93*

Chomsky, N. (1957) *Syntactic Structures*, The Hague, Mouton. *98*

Clowes, M.B. (1971) 'On seeing things', *Artificial Intelligence*, 2, 79–116. *98*

Clutton-Brock, T.H. and Harvey, P.H. (1977) 'Primate ecology and social organization', *Journal of Zoology*, 183, 1–39. *122*

Clutton-Brock, T.H., Albon, S.D., Gibson, R.M. and Guinness, F.E. (1979) 'The logical stag: adaptive aspects of fighting behaviour in red deer (*Cervus elaphs* L.)', *Animal Behaviour*, 27, 211–25. *57*

Cody, M.L. (1971) 'Finch flocks in the Mohave desert', *Theoretical Population Biology*, 2, 142–58. *50*

Collias, N.E., Collias, E.C., Hunsaker, D. and Minning, L. (1966) 'Locality fixation, mobility and social organization within an unconfined population of red jungle fowl', *Animal Behaviour*, 14, 550–59. *63*

Collier, G.H. and Rovee-Collier, C.K. (1981) 'A comparative analysis of optimal foraging behavior: laboratory simulations', in Kamil, A.C. and Sargent, T.D. (eds) *Foraging Behavior*, New York, Garland, 39–76. *92*

Crook, J.H. (1970) 'Social organization and the environment: aspects of contemporary social ethology', *Animal Behaviour*, 18, 197–209. *13, 14*

Daly, M. and Wilson, M. (1981) 'Abuse and neglect of children in evolutionary perspective', in Alexander, R.D. and Tinkle, D.W. (eds) *Natural Selection and Social Behavior*, New York, Chiron, 405–16. *58*

Darwin, C. (1958) *The Autobiography of Charles Darwin*, London, Collins (originally published, 1887). *10*

Dawkins, R. (1976) *The Selfish Gene*, London, Oxford University Press. *77, 114*

Dawkins, R. (1982) *The Extended Phenotype*, Oxford, Freeman. *54*

Dawkins, R. and Krebs, J.R. (1978) 'Animal signals: information or manipulation?', in Krebs, J.R. and Davies, N.B. (eds) *Behavioural Ecology*, Oxford, Blackwell, 282–309. *43, 44*

Deag, J.M. (1977) 'Aggression and submission in monkey societies', *Animal Behaviour*, 25, 465–74. *63*

Dickinson, A. (1981) *Contemporary Animal Learning Theory*, Cambridge, Cambridge University Press. *90*

Dilger, W.C. (1962) 'The behavior of lovebirds', *Scientific American*, 206 (1), 88–98. *41*

Douglas, M. and Isherwood, B. (1979) *The World of Goods*, London, Allen Lane. *120*

Eibl-Eibesfeldt, I. (1975) *Ethology*, 2nd edn, New York, Holt, Rinehart & Winston. *32*

Eibl-Eibesfeldt, I. (1979) *The Biology of Peace and War*, London, Thames & Hudson. *55*

Faaborg, J. and Patterson, C.B. (1981) 'The characteristics and occurrence of cooperative polyandry', *Ibis*, 123, 477–84. *75*

Fenner, F. (1965) 'Myxoma virus and *Oryctolagus cuniculus*: two colonizing species', in Baker, H.G. and Stebbins, G.L. (eds) *The Genetics of Colonizing Species*, New York, Academic Press, 485–501. *53*

Freedman, J.L. (1975) *Crowding and Behavior*, San Francisco, Freeman. *59*

Garcia, J. and Koelling, R.A. (1966) 'Relation of cue to consequence in avoidance learning', *Psychonomic Science*, 4, 123–4. *93*

Gardner, B.T. and Gardner, R.A. (1971) 'Two-way communication with an infant chimpanzee', in Schrier, A.M. and Stollnitz, F. (eds) *Behavior of Nonhuman Primates*, vol. 4, New York, Academic Press, 117–84. *102*

Gause, G.F. (1934) *The Struggle for Existence*, Baltimore, Maryland, Williams & Wilkins. *6*

Geach, P. (1957) *Mental Acts*, London, Routledge & Kegan Paul. *113*

Geer, J.H. and Fuhr, R. (1976) 'Cognitive factors in sexual arousal: the role of distraction', *Journal of Consulting and Clinical Psychology*, 44, 238–43. *33*

Gillan, D.J. (1982) 'Ascent of apes', in Griffin, D.R. (ed.) *Animal Mind – Human Mind*, Berlin, Springer-Verlag, 177–200. *102*

Goldstein, M.C. (1971) 'Stratification, polyandry and family structure in central Tibet', *Southwestern Journal of Anthropology*, 27, 64–74. *120*

Goss-Custard, J.D. (1977) 'The energetics of prey selection by redshank, *Tringa totanus* (L.), in relation to prey density', *Journal of Animal Ecology*, 46, 1–19. *91*

Gosse, P.H. (1857) *Omphalos: An Attempt to Untie the Geological Knot*, London, J. Van Voorst. *10*

Gould, S.J. and Lewontin, R.C. (1979) 'The spandrels of San Marco and the Panglossian paradigm: a critique of the adaptationist programme', *Proceedings of the Royal Society*, Series B 205, 581–98. *7*

Gowaty, P.A. (1982) 'Sexual terms in sociobiology: emotionally evocative and, paradoxically, jargon', *Animal Behaviour*, 30, 630–1. *86*

Gubernick, D.J., Jones, K.C. and Klopfer, P.H. (1979) 'Maternal "imprinting" in goats?', *Animal Behaviour*, 27, 314–15. *81*

Guha, A.S. (1981) *An Evolutionary View of Economic Growth*, Oxford, Clarendon Press. *11*

Hall Sternglantz, S., Gray, J.L. and Murakami, M. (1977) 'Adult preferences for infantile facial features: an ethological approach', *Animal Behaviour*, 25, 108–15. *33*

Hamilton, W.D. (1971) 'Geometry for the selfish herd', *Journal of Theoretical Biology*, 31, 295–311. *51*

Harlow, H.F. and Harlow, M.K. (1965) 'The affectional systems', in Schrier, A.M., Harlow, H.F. and Stollnitz, F. (eds) *Behavior of Nonhuman Primates*, vol. 2, New York, Academic Press, 287–334. *82*

Hayes, K.J. and Hayes, C. (1952) 'Imitation in a home-raised chimpanzee', *Journal of Comparative and Physiological Psychology*, 45, 450–9. *100, 101*

Hayes, K.J. and Nissen, C.H. (1971) 'Higher mental functions of a home-raised chimpanzee', in Schrier, A.M. and Stollnitz, F. (eds) *Behavior of Non-human Primates*, vol. 4, New York, Academic Press, 59–115. *101*

Hediger, H. (1951) *Wild Animals in Captivity*, London, Butterworth. *36*

Herrnstein, R.J. and Loveland, D.H. (1964) 'Complex visual concept in the pigeon', *Science*, 146, 549–51. *100*

Hinde, R.A. (1970) *Animal Behavior*, 2nd edn, New York, McGraw-Hill. *x*

Hinde, R.A. and Spencer-Booth, Y. (1971) 'Effects of brief separation from mother on rhesus monkeys', *Science*, 173, 111–18. *82*

Hirshleifer, J. (1977) 'Economics from a biological viewpoint', *Journal of Law and Economics*, 20, 1–52. *11*

Hrdy, S.B. (1977) *The Langurs of Abu*, Cambridge, Massachusetts, Harvard University Press. *58, 65*

Hull, C.L. (1952) *A Behavior System*, New Haven, Connecticut, Yale University Press. *30*

Humphrey, N.K. (1976) 'The social function of intellect', in Bateson, P.P.G. and Hinde, R.A. (eds) *Growing Points in Ethology*, Cambridge, Cambridge University Press, 303–17. *106*

Huxley, J.S. (1914) 'The courtship-habits of the great crested grebe (*Podiceps cristatus*): with an addition to the theory of natural selection', *Proceedings of the Zoological Society of London*, 1914, 491–562. *39*

Itani, J. (1958) 'On the acquisition and propagation of a new food habit in the natural group of the Japanese monkey at Takasaki-Yama', *Primates*, 1, 84–98. *105*

Itani, J. (1959) 'Paternal care in the wild Japanese monkey, *Macaca fuscata fuscata*', *Primates*, 2, 61–93. *104*

Jenni, D.A. (1974) 'Evolution of polyandry in birds', *American Zoologist*, 14, 129–44. *65, 75*

Jerison, H.J. (1973) *Evolution of the Brain and Intelligence*, New York, Academic Press. *106*

Jolly, A. (1966) 'Lemur social behavior and primate intelligence', *Science*, 153, 501–6. *106*

Jung, C.G. (1966) 'On the psychology of the unconscious', in Jung, C.G., *Collected Works*, vol. 7, 2nd edn, London, Routledge & Kegan Paul, 1–119 (originally published, 1917). *81*

Kellogg, W.N. (1968) 'Communication and language in the home-raised chimpanzee', *Science*, 162, 423–7. *101*

Kenward, E.E. (1978) 'Hawks and doves: attack success and selection in goshawk flights at woodpigeons', *Journal of Animal Ecology*, 47, 449–60. *51*

Klopfer, P.H., Adams, D.K. and Klopfer, M.S. (1964) 'Maternal "imprinting" in goats', *Proceedings of the National Academy of Sciences*, 52, 911–14. *81*

Kohler, W. (1927) *The Mentality of Apes*, 2nd edn, London, Routledge & Kegan Paul. *61*

Konishi, M. and Nottebohm, F. (1969) 'Experimental studies in the ontogeny of avian vocalizations', in Hinde, R.A. (ed.) *Bird Vocalizations*, Cambridge, Cambridge University Press, 29–48. *96*

Krebs, J.R., Kacelnik, A. and Taylor, P. (1978) 'Optimal sampling by birds: an experiment with great tits (*Parus major*)', *Nature*, 275, 27–31. *43, 92*

Kroodsma, D.E. (1977) 'Correlates of song organization among North American wrens', *American Naturalist*, 111, 995–1008. *96*

Kruuk, H. (1972) *The Spotted Hyena*, Chicago, Chicago University Press. *56*

Kuhn, T.S. (1962) *The Structure of Scientific Revolutions*, Chicago, Chicago University Press. *14*

Lack, D. (1954) *The Natural Regulation of Animal Numbers*, Oxford, Clarendon Press. *73, 85*

Lea, S.E.G. (1979) 'Foraging and reinforcement schedules in the pigeon: optimal and non-optimal aspects of choice', *Animal Behaviour*, 27, 875–86. *92*

Lea, S.E.G. (1981) 'Correlation and contiguity in foraging behaviour', in Harzem, P. and Zeiler, M.D. (eds) *Predictability, Correlation and Contiguity*, Chichester, West Sussex, Wiley, 355–406. *92*

Le Roy Ladurie, E. (1980) *Montaillou*, Harmondsworth, Middlesex, Penguin. *61, 62*

Leuze, C.C.K. (1980) 'The application of radio tracking and its effect on the behavioural ecology of the water vole, *Arvicola terrestris* (Lacapede)', in Amlaner, C.J. and Macdonald, D.W. (eds) *A Handbook of Biotelemetry and Radio Tracking*, Oxford, Pergamon, 361–6. *64*

Lévi-Strauss, C. (1966) *The Savage Mind*, London, Weidenfield & Nicolson. *113*

Leyhausen, P. (1973) 'On the function of the relative hierarchy of moods', in Lorenz, K. and Leyhausen, P., *Motivation of Human and Animal Behavior*, New York, Van Nostrand, 144–247 (originally published 1965). *29*

Loiselle, P.V. and Barlow, G.W. (1978) 'Do fishes lek like birds?', in Reese, E.S. and Lighter, F.J. (eds) *Contrasts in Behavior*, New York, Wiley, 31–75. *72*

Lorenz, K.Z. (1950) 'The comparative method in studying innate behaviour patterns', *Symposia of the Society for Experimental Biology*, 4, 219–68. *38*

Lorenz, K.Z. (1958) 'The evolution of behavior', *Scientific American*, 199 (6), 67–78. *42*

Lorenz, K.Z. (1966) *On Aggression*, London, Methuen. *43, 55*

Lorenz, K.Z. (1970a) 'A consideration of methods of identification of species-specific instinctive behaviour patterns in birds', in Lorenz, K., *Studies in Human and Animal Behaviour*, vol. 1, London, Methuen, 57–100 (originally published, 1932). *21*

Lorenz, K.Z. (1970b) 'Companions as factors in the bird's environment', in Lorenz, K., *Studies in Human and Animal Behaviour*, vol. 1, London, Methuen, 101–258 (originally published, 1935). *95*

Lorenz, K.Z. (1970c) 'The establishment of the instinct concept', in Lorenz, K., *Studies in Human and Animal Behaviour*, vol. 1, London, Methuen, 259–315 (originally published, 1937). *25*

Lorenz, K.Z. and Tinbergen, N. (1970) 'Taxis and instinctive behaviour patterns in egg-rolling by the greylag goose', in Lorenz, K., *Studies in Human and Animal Behaviour*, vol. 1, London, Methuen, 316–50 (originally published, 1938). *19*

MacArthur, R.H. and Pianka, E.R. (1966) 'On optimal use of a patchy environment', *American Naturalist*, 100, 603–9. *91*

MacDonald, D.W. (1979) '"Helpers" in fox society', *Nature*, 282, 69–71. *75*

McDougall, W. (1932) *The Energies of Men*, London, Methuen. *19*

McFadden, E.S. and Sears, E.R. (1947) 'The genome approach to radical wheat breeding', *Journal of the American Society of Agronomists*, 39, 1011–26. *10*

MacFarlane, A. (1975) 'Olfaction in the development of social preferences in the human neonate', in Porter, R. and O'Connor, M. (eds) *Parent–Infant Interaction*, Amsterdam, Elsevier, 103–17. *81*

Macphail, E.M. (1982) *Brain and Intelligence in Vertebrates*, Oxford, Clarendon Press. *119*

Malson, L. (1972) *Wolf Children and the Problem of Human Nature*, New York, Monthly Review Press. *98*

Marler, P. (1959) 'Developments in the study of animal communication', in Bell, P.R. (ed.) *Darwin's Biological Work*, London, Cambridge University Press, 150–206. *45*

Matthews, G.V.T. (1968) *Bird Navigation*, Cambridge, Cambridge University Press. *96*

Maynard Smith, J. (1976) 'Evolution and the theory of games', *American Scientist*, 64, 41–5. *57*

Mead, M. (1943) *Coming of Age in Samoa*, Harmondsworth, Middlesex, Penguin. *120*

Mehler, J., Bertoncini, J., Barrière, M. and Jassik-Gerschenfeld, D. (1978) 'Infant recognition of mother's voice', *Perception*, 7, 491–7. *81*

Mehrabian, A. (1972) *Nonverbal Communication*, Chicago, Aldine-Atherton. *47*

Midgley, M. (1979) *Beast and Man*, Brighton, Harvester. *125*

Mitchell, G.D. (1969) 'Paternalistic behavior in primates', *Psychological Bulletin*, 71, 399–417. *83*

Moore, J.R. (1979) *The Post-Darwinian Controversies*, Cambridge, Cambridge University Press. *10*

Morris, D. (1959) 'The comparative ethology of grassfinches (Erythrurae) and mannikins (Amadinae)', *Proceedings of the Zoological Society of London*, 131, 389–439. *37, 40*

Morris, D. (1967) *The Naked Ape*, London, Cape. *27*

Pavlov, I.P. (1927) *Conditioned Reflexes*, London, Oxford University Press. *89*

Perdeck, A.C. (1958) 'Two types of orientation in migrating starlings *Sturnus vulgaris* L. and chaffinches *Fringilla coelebs* L., as revealed by displacement experiments', *Ardea*, 46, 1–37. *96*

Polis, G.A. (1981) 'The evolution and dynamics of intraspecific predation', in Johnson, R.F., Frank, P.W. and Michener, C.D. (eds) *Annual Review of Ecology and Systematics*, vol. 12, Palo Alto, California, Annual Reviews, 225–51. *85*

Popper, K.R. (1959) *The Logic of Scientific Discovery*, London, Hutchinson. *9*

Powell, R. W. and Kelly, W. (1975) 'A method for the objective study of tool-using behavior', *Journal of the Experimental Analysis of Behavior*, 24, 249–53. *99*

Prechtl, H.F.R. (1958) 'The directed head turning response of the human baby', *Behaviour*, 13, 212–42. *32*

Premack, D. (1976) *Intelligence in Ape and Man*, Hillsdale, New Jersey, Erlbaum. *102*

Pryor, K.W., Haag, R. and O'Reilly, J. (1969) 'The creative porpoise: training for novel behavior', *Journal of the Experimental Analysis of Behavior*, 12, 653–61. *101*

Pulliam, H.R. and Dunford, C. (1980) *Programmed to Learn*, New York, Columbia University Press. *104*

Rescorla, R.A. (1967) 'Pavlovian conditioning and its proper control procedures', *Psychological Review*, 74, 71–80. *89*

Reynolds, V. (1980) *The Biology of Human Action*, 2nd edn, Oxford, Freeman. *106*

Richards, M.P.M. (1979) 'Effects on development of medical interventions and the separation of newborns from their parents', in Shaffer, D. and Dunn, J. (eds) *The First Year of Life*, Chichester, West Sussex, Wiley, 37–54. *97*

Rothenbuhler, W.C. (1964) 'Behavior genetics of nest cleaning in honeybees. IV. Responses of F1 and backcross generations to disease-killed brood', *American Zoologist*, 4, 111–23. *41*

Rowell, T.E. (1967) 'A quantitative comparison of the behaviour of a wild and a caged baboon troop', *Animal Behaviour*, 15, 499–509. *51, 63*

Rowell, T.E., Hinde, R.A. and Spencer-Booth, Y. (1964) '"Aunt"–infant interaction in captive rhesus monkeys', *Animal Behaviour*, 12, 219–26. *83*

Rumbaugh, D.M. (1977) *Language Learning by a Chimpanzee*, New York, Academic Press. *102*

Ryan, C.M.E. (1982) 'Mechanisms of individual recognition in birds', unpublished M.Phil. dissertation, University of Exeter. *89*

Ryle, G. (1949) *The Concept of Mind*, London, Hutchinson. *100*

Sade, D.S. (1972) 'Sociometrics of *Macaca mulatta* I. Linkages and cliques in grooming matrices', *Folia Primatologica*, 18, 196–223. *61*

Sahlins, M. (1977) *The Use and Abuse of Biology*, London, Tavistock. *124*

Schaller, G.B. (1972) *The Serengeti Lion*, Chicago, University of Chicago Press. *50, 58*

Schenkel, R. (1947) 'Ausdrucks-Studien an Wolfen', *Behaviour*, 1, 81–129. *47*

Schjelderup-Ebbe, T. (1922) 'Beiträge zur Sozialpsychologie des Haushuhns', *Zeitschrift für Psychologie*, 88, 225–52. *63*

Seligman, M.E.P. (1970) 'On the generality of the laws of learning', *Psychological Review*, 77, 406–18. *94*

Seligman, M.E.P. (1971) 'Phobias and preparedness', *Behavior Therapy*, 2, 307–20. *94*

Shettleworth, S.J. (1975) 'Reinforcement and the organization of behaviour in golden hamsters: hunger, environment and food reinforcement', *Journal of Experimental Psychology: Animal Behaviour Processes*, 1, 56–87. *22, 94*

Shettleworth, S.J. (1983) 'Memory in food-hoarding birds', *Scientific American*, 248 (3), 86–94. *93*

Skinner, B.F. (1938) *The Behavior of Organisms*, New York, Appleton-Century-Crofts. *90*

Skinner, B.F. (1962) 'Two "synthetic social relations"', *Journal of the Experimental Analysis of Behavior*, 5, 531–3. *99*

Skinner, B.F. (1969) *Contingencies of Reinforcement*, New York, Appleton-Century-Crofts. *90, 112*

Small, W.S. (1900–1) 'Experimental studies of the mental processes of the rat II', *American Journal of Psychology*, 12, 206–39. *89, 90*

Stanley, S.M. (1975) 'A theory of evolution above the species level', *Proceedings of the National Academy of Sciences of the USA*, 72, 646–50. *54*

Suomi, S.J. and Harlow, H.F. (1972) 'Depressive behavior in young monkeys subjected to vertical chamber confinement', *Journal of Comparative and Physiological Psychology*, 80, 11–18. *82*

Symons, D. (1979) *The Evolution of Human Sexuality*, New York, Oxford University Press. *121*

Tarpy, R.M. and Sawabini, F.L. (1974) 'Reinforcement delay: a selective review of the last decade', *Psychological Bulletin*, 81, 984–97. *93*

Terrace, H.S. (1979) *Nim*, New York, Knopf. *102*

Thielcke, G. (1969) 'Geographic variation in bird vocalizations', in Hinde R.A. (ed.) *Bird Vocalizations*, Cambridge, Cambridge University Press, 311–39. *96*

Thompson, T.I. (1963) 'Visual reinforcement in Siamese fighting fish', *Science*, 141, 55–7. *90*

Thorndike, E.L. (1898) 'Animal intelligence', *Psychological Review Monographs* 2, (8). *90*

Thorndike, E.L. (1913) *Educational Psychology*, vol. 2: *The Psychology of Learning*, New York, Teachers' College, Columbia University. *30*

Thunberg, B.E. (1971) 'Olfaction in parent stream selection by the alewife (*Alosa pseudoharengus*)', *Animal Behaviour*, 19, 217–25. *95*

Tinbergen, N. (1948) 'Dierkundeles in het meeuwenduin', *De Levende Natuur*, 51, 49–56. *24*

Tinbergen, N. (1951) *The Study of Instinct*, Oxford, Clarendon Press. *19, 39, 54*

Tinbergen, N. (1959) 'Comparative studies of the behaviour of gulls (Laridae)', *Behaviour*, 15, 1–70. *55*

Tinbergen, N. and Perdeck, A.C. (1950) 'On the stimulus situation releasing the begging response in the newly-hatched herring-gull chick (*Larus argentatus* Pont.)', *Behaviour*, 3, 1–39. *24*

Trivers, R.L. (1974) 'Parent-offspring conflict', *American Zoologist*, 14, 249–64. *85*

Turnbull, C. (1973) *The Mountain People*, London, Cape. *119*

Van Hooff, J.A.R.A.M. (1962) 'Facial expressions in higher primates', *Symposia of the Zoological Society of London*, 8, 97–125. *47*

Van Lawick-Goodall, J. (1974) *In the Shadow of Man*, London, Fontana. *82*

Von Frisch, K. (1926) 'Vergleichende Physiologie des Geruchs- und Geschmackssinnes', in Bethe, A., von Bergmann, G., Embden, G. and Ellinger, A. (eds) *Handbuch der normalen und pathologischen Physiologie*, vol. II, Part I, Berlin, Springer, 203–40. *70*

Von Frisch, K. (1966) *The Dancing Bees*, 2nd edn, London, Methuen. *50*

Washburn, S.L. and DeVore, I. (1961) 'The social life of baboons', *Scientific American*, 204 (6), 62–71. *51*

Watts, C.R. and Stokes, A.W. (1971) 'The social order of turkeys', *Scientific American*, 224 (6), 112–18. *65*

Williams, M. (1979) *Brain Damage, Behaviour and the Mind*, Chichester, West Sussex, Wiley. *98*

Wilson, E.O. (1975) *Sociobiology*, Cambridge, Massachusetts, Harvard University Press. *14, 49*

Wittgenstein, L. (1968) *Philosophical Investigations*, 3rd edn, Oxford, Blackwell (originally published, 1953). *100*

Wolf, L.L. (1975) 'Energy intake and expenditure in a nectar-feeding sunbird', *Ecology*, 56, 92–104. *66*

Wrangham, R.W. (1979) 'On the evolution of ape social systems', *Social Science Information*, 18, 335–68. *66*

Yeaton, R.I. and Cody, M.L. (1974) 'Competitive release in island song sparrow populations', *Theoretical Population Biology*, 5, 42–58. *73*

Subject index

The references section of this book serves as a name index. Names are included in this index only where there is no corresponding literature citation; in most cases these are the names of historical personages. Italicized page numbers indicate where commonly used terms are defined.

conditioning, 89, 106, 112; classical, 89–90; instrumental, 89–90; operant, 89–90, 102, 111; Pavlovian, 89–90
conflict of drives, 35–7, 40 (*see also* approach–avoid conflict)
connectionism, 30
consciousness, 18, 19, 32, 110
constraints on learning, 93–5
contact species, 36, 61
contests, in mating, 72
contingency-governed behaviour, 112
contour, as a perceptual quality, 25
controlled mating, 41
copulation, 36, 70, 74, 101, 115 (*see also* breeding, mating)
core area, 64
cost-benefit analysis, 49, 57, 69, 78, 86
courtship, 38, 40, 42, 44, 71, 77, 79, 128; male display in, 70–3
Craig, W., 13
creationism, 5
critical period, 95
cross-breeding, 10
crow, 99, 106
crypsis: *see* camouflage
cuckoo, 12, 70, 85, 96
cultural evolution, 12, 16, 104, 114, 129; vs. genetic evolution, 114–16
cultural selection vs. genetic selection, 116, 122
cultural transmission of behaviour, 96, 103–5
culture, 11, 32, Chapter 6, 113, *114*, 117–18, 123; animal, 96, 129; human, 120; pool of ideas that constitute, 116
cultures, differences between, 110, 119

Darwin, C., 5, 8–11, 13
Dawkins, R., 14
deafness, 98, 102; congenital, 113
deceit, 46, 103, 107
defence of territory, 15, 27–9, 43, 62–3, 66–7, 72–3, 75, 77
delay of reinforcement, 93
delinquency in human juveniles, 122
deprivation, 29; maternal, 82–3, 129; of peers, 82–3; sensory, 82
determinism, biological, 116

dialects in birdsong, 96
discrimination: colours, 24; concepts, 100, 113
disease, 41, 53
displacement reaction, 36–40, 61, 71, 125
display: aggressive, 42–3, 47, 55, 60, 62–3, 90; by males in courtship, 70–3; ecstatic, 62; mutual, 62
distance species, 35, 38–9, 61, 115
distribution of animals, 66, 70, 73 (*see also* territory)
diurnal variations, 66
division of labour, sexual, 120
DNA, 109, 115
dog, 89
dolphin, 111
dominance, 62–3, 120; hierarchy, 63, 125; of one sex over the other, 61–2, 123–4; relationships, 62, 64, 107
dove, 59
Dow, S. M., 92
drive, 18, 27–31, 35, 37, 94 (*see also* aggression, fear, hunger, mating, parenting, sex); conflict of, 35–7, 40 (*see also* approach–avoid conflict)
ducks, 20, 42, 80, 117

ecological niche, 6, 7, 41
ecology, 15, 49, 109, 121; island, 99
economics, 112; 'free market', 10
ecstatic display of penguins, 62
egg, 25, 33, 39, 48, 69, 71, 75, 77, 79, 85, 96; retrieval by greylag goose, 19–23
egocentric speech, 103
elephant, 54
elephant seal, 70, 71
emancipation of fixed action patterns, 38–40
endocrine system, 28
energy: action specific, 30; as a cost of behaviour, 66, 69–71
environment: external vs. internal, 28; social, 14
environmental psychology, 4
ethologists, 12–13, 19, 40, 60, 73
ethology, *1*; applied, 3–5, 16; comparative, 12–14, 16, 54, 60, 125,

grass finch, 40, 48
great tit, 63, 92
greylag goose, 18–23, 80, 96
grooming: *see* care of the body surface;
   social function of, 61
group: defence, 51; selection, 52–4, 73
   (*see also* good of the species)
gull, ix, 3, 26, 36, 72 (*see also* herring
   gull, kittiwake)

habituation, *89*–90, 106
hair, human, 62, 108
hamadryas baboon, 65, 71
hamster, 22, 94
hand, human, 109
Hanuman langur, 58–9, 65, 75
harem, 57, 74, 76–8
hawk, 45, 51, 77
hedgehog, 36
Heinroth, O., 13
'helpers at the nest', 84
heritability of behaviour, 71
heron, 42
herring gull, 20, 23–6, 28–9, 42–4, 48,
   55–6, 64, 80–1, 85
hierarchy, of dominance relationships,
   48, 63, 125
higher-order response classes, 101
home range, 44
homing, 96, 98, 106
honey bee, 50
hormones, 28–9, 33
hornbill, 75
horse, 54
howler monkey, 64
human: adaptability, 109; behaviour, 3,
   16, 33, 36–7, 41, 46–7, 51, 58, 61,
   82–4, 106, Chapter 7: aggression, 55,
   59–60, 110, 122, appeasement,
   59–60, delousing, 61–2, instincts,
   32, 60, 124, 128 (evolutionarily
   conservative, 116–18), intelligence,
   100, 125 (evolution, 105–7),
   language: *see* language, 'natural', 70,
   83, 86, 121, sex roles, 86–7, signals,
   46–7, tool use, 110; brain, 108, 111,
   118, evolution, 106; breast, 26–7, 32;
   capacity to reason and plan ahead,

18, 112, 119; culture, 120; ethology, 4
   (*see also* human behaviour); hand,
   109; mother-infant bonding, 81, 124;
   nature, 125; societies, 86, 110, 120;
   sociobiology, 129; special learning
   abilities, 97–9; uniqueness, 3, 17, 55,
   87, Chapter 7, 125; voice, 81
humans, as fitting into a biological
   pattern, 118–22
hummingbird, 63, 66
hunger (drive), 29–31, 35
hunter-gatherer societies, 106, 120
hunting, 27, 119 (*see also* foraging);
   -dog, 111; of cats, 30; social, 106–7,
   113
Huxley, J., 13
hybrids, 41–2, 71; infertility, 42, 71
hyena, 56
hygienic bees, 41
Hymenoptera, 49, 84 (*see also* ant, bee,
   wasp)

ideas, 114–15
Ik, 119
imitation, 90, 101, 103, 106, 114; set,
   100, 103
implication chain, 120
imprinting, 80, 86, 95, 97
incest taboo, 11
individual distance, 4, 36, 125 (*see also*
   distance species)
individual recognition, 80–1, 87, 89, 95
individual selection, 52–4
infanticide, 8, 58, 60, 75
infertility of hybrids, 42, 71
information, 88, 103, 113
inheritance of instincts, 40–2
innate releasing mechanism (IRM),
   31–2, 34–5, 39–42, 55, 62, 71, 99, 105;
   evolution of, 58
instinct, 16, Chapter 2, 78, 81, 91–2,
   116, 119; deviations from, 39;
   evolution of, Chapter, 3; human, 32,
   60, 124, 128; inheritance, 40–2; vs.
   learning, 91
instrumental conditioning, 89–90
intelligence, 18, 32, Chapter 6, 98;
   animal, 99–101; human, 100, 135;

ego, 110; importance of biology to, 2–3; relation of ethology to, 4; social, 4, 36, 46, 59, 110
punctuated equilibria in evolution, 7
purposive behaviour, 90

rabbit, 42, 45, 53
'race to desert' offspring, 77, 86
radical behaviourism, 112
rat, 3, 36, 37, 56, 61, 90, 92–3
rate of reproduction, 53 (see also fitness, selective advantage)
reason, 18, 112, 119
reasoning: analogical, 102; verbal, 119
recognition, individual, 80–1, 87, 89, 95
red deer, 57, 70, 71, 74
red jungle fowl, 63
redshank, 91
reinforcement, 90, 93; delay of, 93; schedules of, 92
releaser, 25–8, 39, 71, 89
religion, 10, 111; animistic, 111
reproduction, rate of, 53 (see also fitness, selective advantage)
reproductive success: see fitness, selective advantage
resources, 16, 76, 78, 84, 121; limiting, 66
response shaping, Skinnerian, 99
reward, 90, 99, 101; food, 16, 22, 91, 94, 100
rhesus monkey, 61, 82, 122–3, 129
ritualization of fixed action patterns, 38–40, 42, 61, 72
robin (European), 20, 42–3, 62, 73
roles, 48, 50 (see also sex roles)
rough-toothed porpoise, 101
rule-governed behaviour, 112

salivation, 89
saltation, 9
sameness, concept of, 100
scent marking, 22, 70 (see also chemical communication, pheromones)
schedules of reinforcement, 92
science, history of, 14; revolutions in, 14
sea otter, 99

seal, 36, 70–1
seasonal variations in behaviour, 28, 57
selection: cultural vs. genetic, 116, 122; gene, 66 (see also selfish gene theory); group, 52–4; kin, 45, 52–4, 65, 83, 84, 128; level at which it is effective, 52–4; species, 54
selective advantage, 38, 40, 57, 59, 78
selective pressure, 6, 38, 44, 53–4, 56, 58, 69–70, 79, 80, 86, 92, 106, 111, 123; genetic and cultural compared, 117, 121, 123, 125
'selfish gene' theory, 43, 52, 85, 115, 116
sensitive period, 80, 95, 97
sensory deprivation, 82
serial polygamy, 121
sex differences: behaviour, 3, 51, 68 (see also sex roles); body, 74, 79, 121–2; in dominance, 61–2, 123–4
sex: drive, 30, 36, 38; roles, 50–1, 61, 64, 70, 75–6, 78, 83, 118–20, and division of labour, 120, human, 86–7
sexes: conflicting interests of, 44, 125; definition of, 68–70; relationships between, 16, 36, 38–9, 51, 64, Chapter 5, 70, 74, 86, 119
sexual: aggressiveness, 46; attraction, 26; dimorphism, 74, 79, 121–2; partners, 58 (see also mates, pairs); presentation, 56; reproduction, 50, 68; satiation, 122; skin, 56; variety, 122
shaping of responses (Skinnerian), 99
Siamese fighting fish, 63, 74, 77, 90
sibling: group, 65, 75, 121; rivalry, 8, 85
sign language, 111
sign stimuli, 23–6, 28–31, 38–9, 90
signalling instincts, 39, 42–4, 46, 48, 55, 61, 63, 70–1, 79, 128
skill learning, 99
Skinner box, 90, 92, 94, 99
sleep, 27, 37
smell, 81
smiling, 47
social: environment, 14; ethology, 14–15, 125; groups, 58–9, 64; hunting, 51, 106–7, 113; insects, 49; philosophy, 11; primates, 60; psychology, 4, 36, 46, 59, 110;

science, 1; status, 47, 61; structure, 15, 67, 68, 70, 74, 86; structures, complex, 64–5; structures, simple, 62–4
sociobiology, 7, 14, 15, 16, 43, 54, 69, 116, 123, 127; human, 129
solitary animals, 70, 74, 80
song in birds, 28, 55, 96, 98, 103, 108
song sparrow, 72, 96
soul, 110–11
speciation, 9
species (see also contact species, distance species, good of the species): definition of, 6; endangered, 4; selection, 54
species-specific learning abilities, 97–9
specula, 42, 117
speculation, 3, 5
speech, 102; egocentric, 103
sperm, 69, 77
spider monkey, 41, 118
spotted hyena, 56
stepparents, 58
stereotyped behaviour, 20–1
stickleback, 20, 28–9, 39, 42, 55, 62, 74, 77, 83, 90, 122–3
stimulus-response bonds, 30
striated finch, 40, 115
submissiveness, 27, 60, 62–3
subsong, 96
sunbird, 66
super-releaser, 24, 28, 33
survival of the fittest, 6, 11
symmetry, 100

taboos: food, 118; incest, 11
Tasmanian native hen, 75–7
taste, 93 (see also chemical communication)
taxonomy, 20
technology, 60, 110, 120
teeth, 117
territory, 15, 23, 27–9, 43, 62–3, 66, 72–5, 77, 79; defence, 15, 27–9, 43, 62–3, 66–7, 72–3, 75, 77; nested, 64, 75–6
testicles, 74

testosterone, 28
theory of games, 57
threat display, 42–3, 47, 55, 60, 62–3, 90
threat, open-mouthed, 47
thumbs, 41, 109
Tinbergen, N., 13
titi, 83
titmouse: see blue tit, great tit, marsh tit
tools, 99–100; spontaneous use by animals, 99; use by human, 110
'top-down' explanation, 48
trial and error learning, 19
turkey, 65, 121

Uganda kob, 72, 104
unconscious processes, 18, 19, 32, 81, 114
unrestrained aggression, 55, 58–9
upright threat response of herring gull, 55–6

verbal reasoning, 18, 112, 119
vertebrate, 2
virus, 53, 69
vocabulary, 113
vocal tract, 102, 125
vole, 27–8

waggle dance, 50
walking, 47
washing: see care of body surface
water vole, 64
waterbuck, 50
weaning, 86
weapon, 60, 110, 111
Whitman, C. O., 13
wild children, 98
wild rat, 93
wildebeeste, 50
willow warbler, 108
Wilson, E. O., 4
wolf, 47, 59, 106
wood pigeon, 51
woodpecker finch, 99

zebra, 50
zebra finch, 37, 40
zigzag dance of stickleback, 39
zoo animals, 3, 4, 63
zoology, 1, 13, 20, 34–5